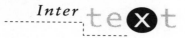

The Language of Children

The INTERTEXT series has been specifically designed to meet the needs of contemporary English Language Studies. *Working with Texts: A core intro-duction to language analysis* (second edition, 2001) is the foundation text, which is complemented by a range of 'satellite' titles. These provide students with hands-on practical experience of textual analysis through special topics and can be used individually or in conjunction with *Working with Texts*.

The Language of Children:

- focuses on the language produced by children, and includes a wide variety of authentic data, from records of children's first words to emails;

- introduces the student to ways of analysing data, from multimodal texts to transcripts of talk during play;

- explores the language of children from a range of backgrounds and abilities;

- reviews key theories of language acquisition;

- provides a historical overview of the subject;

- is user-friendly and accessible, with a helpful glossary;

- suggests significant sources for further study.

Julia Gillen is a Lecturer in Applied Language Studies at the Open University, UK.

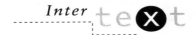

The Intertext series

◎ Why does the phrase 'spinning a yarn' refer both to using language and making cloth?

◎ What might a piece of literary writing have in common with an advert or a note from the milkman?

◎ Which aspects of language are important to understand when analysing texts?

The Routledge INTERTEXT series aims to develop readers' understanding of how texts work. It does this by showing some of the designs and patterns in the language from which they are made, by placing texts within the contexts in which they occur, and by exploring relationships between them.

The series consists of a foundation text, *Working with Texts: A core introduction to language analysis*, which looks at language aspects essential for the analysis of texts, and a range of satellite texts. These apply aspects of language to a particular topic area in more detail. They complement the core text and can also be used alone, providing the user has the foundation skills furnished by the core text.

Benefits of using this series:

◎ **Multi-disciplinary** – provides a foundation for the analysis of texts, supporting students who want to achieve a detailed focus on language.

◎ **Accessible** – no previous knowledge of language analysis is assumed, just an interest in language use.

◎ **Student-friendly** – contains activities relating to texts studied, commentaries after activities, highlighted key terms, suggestions for further reading and an index of terms.

◎ **Interactive** – offers a range of task-based activities for both class use and individual study.

◎ **Tried and tested** – written by a team of respected teachers and practitioners whose ideas and activities have been trialled independently.

The series editors:

Adrian Beard was until recently Head of English at Gosforth High School, and now works at the University of Newcastle upon Tyne. He is a Chief Examiner for AS- and A-Level English Literature. He has written and lectured extensively on the subjects of literature and language. His publications include *Texts and Contexts* (Routledge).

Angela Goddard is Senior Lecturer in Language at the Centre for Human Communication, Manchester Metropolitan University, and is Chair of Examiners for A-Level English Language. Her publications include *Researching Language* (second edition, Heinemann, 2000).

Core textbook:
Working with Texts: A core introduction to language analysis
(second edition, 2001)
Ronald Carter, Angela Goddard, Danuta Reah, Keith Sanger and
Maggie Bowring

Satellite titles:

Language and Gender
Angela Goddard and Lindsey Meân
Patterson

The Language of Advertising: Written texts
(second edition, 2002)
Angela Goddard

The Language of Conversation
Francesca Pridham

The Language of Drama
Keith Sanger

The Language of Fiction
Keith Sanger

The Language of Humour
Alison Ross

*The Language of ICT: Information and
Communication Technology*
Tim Shortis

The Language of Magazines
Linda McLoughlin

The Language of Newspapers
(second edition, 2002)
Danuta Reah

The Language of Poetry
John McRae

The Language of Politics
Adrian Beard

The Language of Speech and Writing
Sandra Cornbleet and Ronald Carter

The Language of Sport
Adrian Beard

The Language of Television
Jill Marshall and Angela Werndly

Related titles:

Child Language
(second edition, 1999)
Jean Peccei

*Child Language: A resource book for
students*
(forthcoming)
Jean Peccei

The Language of Children

◎   Julia Gillen

Routledge
Taylor & Francis Group

LONDON AND NEW YORK

First published 2003
by Routledge
11 New Fetter Lane, London EC4P 4EE

Simultaneously published in the USA and Canada
by Routledge
29 West 35th Street, New York, NY 10001

Routledge is an imprint of the Taylor & Francis Group

© 2003 Julia Gillen

Typeset in Stone Sans/Stone Serif by
Florence Production Ltd, Stoodleigh, Devon
Printed and bound in Great Britain by
TJ International, Padstow, Cornwall

British Library Cataloguing in Publication Data
A catalogue record for this book is available from the British Library

Library of Congress Cataloging in Publication Data
A catalog record for this book has been requested

ISBN 0–415–28620–4 (hbk)
ISBN 0–415–28621–2 (pbk)

For Edgar Rabone

contents

acknowledgements

We are grateful to Charmian Kenner for permission to use material from the project 'Signs of Difference: how children learn to write in different script systems'. The project is funded by the ESRC Award No. R000238456 (2000–2002) (Charmian Kenner and Gunther Kress). We gratefully acknowledge permission from the Open University Press to reproduce an extract from *Promoting Children's Learning from Birth to Five* by Angela Anning and Anne Edwards (1999) on p. 74 and Multilingual Matters for permission to reproduce the text and cartoon on p. 96 (artwork redrawn) from *The Bilingual Family Newsletter* vol. 17 no. 3, p. 3 (2000). Jackie Dennis and Jane Cobb are thanked for assistance in data collection.

Every effort has been made to contact copyright holders for their permission to reprint material in this book. The publishers would be grateful to hear from any copyright holder who is not here acknowledged and will undertake to rectify any errors or omissions in future editions of this book.

Setting the scene

Children's communicative practices are perhaps more varied today than they have ever been. Writing and designing visual images have been extended through new tools and communication channels such as computers and developments in telephone capabilities. Even children who were traditionally highly disadvantaged, such as deaf children, are in some circumstances receiving new opportunities through such technologies and the spread of sign languages. However, for the caregivers of most children, the most significant means of children's participation in human society is speech.

How do children learn to talk? This is a fundamental question driving child language research. Possible answers have been put forward from as early as the fourth century. Saint Augustine (397) entitled a chapter of his *Confessions* (i.e. autobiography) 'That When a Boy He Learned to Speak, Not by Any Set Method, But from the Acts and Words of His Parents':

> So it was that by frequently hearing words, in duly placed sentences, I gradually gathered what things they were the signs of; and having formed my mouth to the utterance of these signs, I thereby expressed my will. Thus I exchanged with those about me the signs by which we express our wishes, and advanced deeper into the stormy fellowship of human life.

In this book you will be presented with plenty of information about children's language development. The intention is to get you thinking about this remarkable phenomenon. It may surprise you to learn that, even after more than a century of scientific study of children's language from infancy, it still remains a controversial arena in terms of theories of how children learn.

There are a number of different ways in which 'the language of children' could be understood. It might mean language used *to* children, such as nursery rhymes and children's literature. This book, however, in common with others in this series, will focus on a particular field, the language that children *use*. This book is about spontaneous language production, that is language that children use to communicate and express themselves in the world. The data – samples of language use – come from children's own language as observed in their own worlds, rather than through laboratory or any other kind of test performance.

With the help of this book you will be equipped to make your own observations of young children's language, and formulate some of your own ideas about what is happening and why.

STARTING POINTS IN INVESTIGATING CHILDREN'S LANGUAGE

As Augustine realised, an appealing, simple explanation as to how children learn to talk is that children imitate what they hear. But if you have had any experience of spending time with young children, you might already have realised that such an explanation would be overly simplistic.

One example is that many young children use the word 'goed' instead of 'went'. For example they say 'I goed to the park', instead of 'I went to the park'. Why?

It seems that young children brought up in English-speaking environments often come to realise (quite unconsciously) that many past tenses in English end in '-ed' (pronounced with a 't' or 'd' sound of course) e.g. 'walked' or 'loaded'. They form, quite unconsciously, a rule for themselves that past tenses end in 'ed' and then overgeneralise that rule. That is, they apply it to verbs which have irregular forms such as 'go' and 'bring'. So they often go through a long stage of saying 'goed' and 'bringed' before eventually learning the actual irregular forms: 'went' and 'brought'.

Interestingly, very young children (perhaps in their second year) often go through a short initial stage of using the correct form 'went' before they start using 'goed'. Presumably, the early correct use comes from simple imitation, but is then replaced by the application of a rule.

This common example is enough then on its own to illustrate that language is not learned through imitation alone, although undoubtedly it plays a part. Important aspects of language learning do happen in the learner's head – these are **cognitive processes**. We need to recognise that these play a part in language learning.

Some theories of child language development concentrate on a **developmental trajectory**. That is, they seek above all to explain how **infants** start off by saying nothing, and after several years come to speak in almost as elaborate ways as adults. Many **psycholinguists** (those psychologists who specialise in language development) try to seek out general patterns in children's acquisition of language and make universal rules as to stages in language development. Such researchers generally adopt a *cognitive* approach, that is they focus on what is going on in the brain of the individual. Their work has been very useful in uncovering interesting patterns in certain groups at least, such as the common movement from 'went' to 'goed' to 'went' described above.

However, many such findings, coming as they do from experimental studies, are governed by the search for factors in common across individuals, and seek to explain language development as a kind of **universal trajectory** from A to B. Traditionally, books on child language development begin at infancy and carry on through the ages and stages identified until a certain age – say school entry. There is a problem with this approach, in that it implies a *deficit model* of child language. That is, what is always emphasised is what children *can't* do. Obviously, it appears, according to that way of thinking, that babies are born without knowing how to communicate and end up as good speakers, readers and writers. So study of language development is seen as a path from a complete deficit position of incapability to that of the perfectly competent adult.

One aim of this book is to urge you to open your eyes to complexity and diversity in children's language use. Other books in this series have shared this aim in respect of other fields of language, such as those of advertising, sport or gender differences. The perspective taken in this book is primarily **sociocultural.** This term will return later; at this point it is used simply to emphasise the significance of the varying social contexts in which language is used and learned. All of us are born into and live in a slightly different societal niche; even in the same family the experience of the youngest child will be different from the oldest. It is therefore not surprising that our experiences and uses of language will be subtly different from everyone else's.

Let us now consider two examples from the talk of two-year-old children.

Example 1: Leon

Leon is aged 2′ 6″ (this is the convention in child language studies for indicating '2 years and 6 months') and is being brought up bilingually – his mother is a native German and his father a native Irishman who has lived in Germany. The family live in England and from an early age Leon has been spending time with other caregivers who speak only English. Leon's parents speak to him in German only. Up to this point Leon had seemed relatively late in starting to speak at all, and often spoke in something of a mixture between the two languages. If he did use a statement in only English or German, it sometimes seemed to onlookers a matter of luck as to whether it was directed to an English or German speaker.

Activity

Look at the account in Text: Leon and describe Leon's linguistic competencies (skills in language) that are shown here.

Text: Leon

One morning a visiting friend of his mother was in the bathroom. Leon shouted through the locked door:
'Julia, what doing?'
Julia replied, 'I'm cleaning my teeth.'
Leon then went downstairs to the kitchen and said to his mother,
'Julia putzt zähne' ('Julia brushing teeth', in German).

Commentary

This incident is notable because it shows that Leon understands that one language is appropriate for some interlocutors (people he talks with) and another for others. He first posed a question in English and received a response in English. His most notable achievement was that he then acted as a translator. That is, he heard a statement in English and converted it to German, the language of his mother. This means that he is sorting out language into two different systems, recognising that objects have two labels and that more complex phrases can be expressed in different yet equivalent ways. At the time his mother was indeed astonished and delighted as this was the first time she had heard him clearly translate a statement from one language to another.

Example 2: Nadia

Activity

What does Nadia's **utterance** (segment of speech) below demonstrate about her communicative competencies?

Text: Nadia

Nadia, 2′ 5″, picked up a toy telephone. She said into it, fairly rapidly, 'Hello, hello, bye, see you later', and put the phone down again.

Commentary

Nadia knows that the telephone, unlike most household objects, elicits talk. She understands that this toy is a replica of such instruments. From the short description above, we cannot tell whether Nadia understood that other voices are usually on the other end of telephones, or whether they are simply things to be talked into (as you might think if you only ever witnessed one end of calls). What she chooses to say into the phone is interesting. In actual telephone calls, greetings and farewells are almost always a strong feature. This is because beginnings and ends

5

of conversations are absolute and distinct (unlike in face-to-face talk) and cannot be made less abrupt through non-verbal communication. So it is usual to mark clearly the two ends of a call. Research has shown that pretence calls by very young children demonstrate that children have noticed this, in that these features tend often to constitute their early telephone play.

TOWARDS A SOCIOCULTURAL APPROACH TO LANGUAGE DEVELOPMENT

One implication of the 'deficit model' of child language development is the proposal that adults' language represents an ideal level of competence.

Activity

Make brief notes on the following questions and compare with someone else if possible.

◎ Are you equally competent in all areas of English (e.g. writing essays, public speaking, emailing etc.)?

◎ Do you have competence in any other language?

◎ Do you always speak in the same style, whoever you are talking to?

◎ Have you recently joined a new group of some kind in which you were faced with new terminology or jargon? (Perhaps through work, sport or a hobby?)

Commentary

Obviously people's answers to the above questions will vary tremendously. Actually that's part of the point of this exercise – to suggest that adult's language use is very diverse rather than being an ideal competence which children, viewed in an equally simplistic way, simply do not match up to.

Very likely, you can think of aspects of English activity you are less good at than others. Perhaps you are less quick and successful at telling jokes than your friends, or perhaps find writing essays challenging. You might well be bilingual, having at least some knowledge of more than one language. However there are many people in monolingual societies who go through their lives without ever translating a sentence into another language in the way that Leon did, as reported in this unit. (It should be pointed out though that more people in the world live in bilingual than in monolingual societies.)

Even if you don't speak another language it is highly likely that you modify your language to suit different settings. Perhaps you are conscious that you speak rather differently when talking with someone in authority such as a headteacher or doctor, than you do when chatting with your friends. Even if you are convinced this is not true of you, would you still speak in the same way to a five-year-old child or a foreigner with poor English asking you directions?

One of the situations that often causes some language gains or modification is joining a new society. 'Society' does not necessarily only mean either moving to a new area or even joining a formal club, but rather starting a new activity which has its own ways of speaking. These might include technical terms, jargon or simply informal conversational shortcuts that operate in a particular group. If you have worked in a part-time job, you might well have noticed you were learning new ways of speaking (or writing) that accompanied the new activities.

So, adults' language is extremely diverse, influenced by all sorts of experiences that have happened to them and the different kinds of settings in which they use language.

So one important way in which a sociocultural approach turns away from the 'deficit model' of child language development is in its emphasis of diversity in children's language use. The 'Leon' and 'Nadia' texts above gave good examples of how considering a specific utterance from a two-year-old child can be enough to question any assumption that children follow a universal path in language learning – from 'nowhere' to 'the ideal'.

Activity

Think of any children under eight that you know. (If you don't know any, you will have to try and remember your own early childhood.)

◎   Can they express themselves?

◎   Do you generally understand what they want?

◎   What limitations are obvious in their communicative abilities?

Commentary

Even babies are generally very good at expressing their immediate needs (food, discomfort etc.). Some carers recognise different cries even in very young children. In Unit five, Communication before language, you will find evidence that babies communicate to interact with other people, that is to cement their relationships, play games and so on. Toddlers and young children are generally extremely good at expressing their immediate wishes, as is very well known! Indeed, we will be looking in Unit four at how they can create quite complex meanings even when they are at the 'one-word stage'.

It would be foolish to pretend that a young child's language is anything like as flexible as your own. You may have picked on any one of a number of areas of limitation. Young children's **phonological** system, that is the way they pronounce words, can be very individualised. They can be hard to understand, especially by those less familiar with them. The meaning they attach to words (**semantic** understanding) may be quite different from the conventionalised meanings that can be found in dictionaries. Indeed their **lexicon** (vocabulary) will be smaller. Children's grammatical constructions (**syntax**) might be restricted in complexity. Once a child learns to use 'because' appropriately for example, a whole host of logical relations becomes possible to express that previously were difficult if not impossible to explain and thus perhaps even to think about. One especial difference is that young children are unlikely to operate with the same variety of **semiotic** systems as you. School students are likely to operate with mathematical symbols, musical notes, fine art conventions etc. as well as many different written **genres**. In their broader lives they can interpret verbal and image-based puns on posters, appreciate the conventions of music videos and so on. Although we have all heard of gifted young mathematicians, musicians and writers, most young children are of course *relatively* less experienced in the immense range of communications present in our culture. In general, school is important for most of us in facilitating the learning of skills in new communication channels such as the written word and the mathematical symbol system.

One goal of asking you to think about adults' diversity in language use first, was partly to emphasise that children's language is varied too. Furthermore, if we are prepared to recognise them, the competencies of children virtually from birth can be extremely impressive, as shall be demonstrated further in this book.

SUMMARY

In this unit we have established that:

◎ Imitation is inadequate as a complete explanation for how children learn to talk.

◎ Children's communicative experiences are extremely varied in terms of languages and tools to which they have access.

◎ Children's communicative practices are also varied, influenced by their culture and society.

◎ An assumption that children's language learning is an even progress along a path from knowing nothing to complete 'adult competence' is too simplistic, partly because adults vary so much in their linguistic practices.

◎ Young children's linguistic capabilities have considerable limitations in many aspects.

HOW TO USE THIS BOOK

The remainder of the book is organised into themes, so that if you are interested in one particular area, first words, say, you can go straight to that chapter rather than read the book in order. If you do choose to read it from the beginning to the end though, you will notice that more information about older children appears at the beginning of the book and the youngest feature most in the penultimate unit. This reversal of the traditional order seeks to emphasise that at all times language development is founded upon earlier experiences that can be investigated themselves in turn.

Technical terms appear in **bold** the first time they are used. Those that are not defined at the point of being used, or are used more than once, receive explanation in the Index of terms on p. 97. Suggestions for further research work appear in 'Ideas for further projects' on p. 89. If you would like to follow up any issues in further detail, you will find some recommended books and other sources of material on pp. 91–2, 93–6.

Writing and multimodality

Language in any form is a system of symbols. Whether we speak or write we make use of sounds or graphics that are conventionally agreed to stand for certain meanings. Yet the description of language as a 'code' is inadequate, for in practice it is never a single symbolic system existing in isolation. In this unit we will see various ways in which symbolic practices exist in interplay, perhaps of words with visual images, certainly of any symbol as it is interpreted against the background of its context. We will consider various ways in which children's language is produced **multimodally**.

This book does not directly discuss the learning of reading. As explained in Unit one, rather than taking a cognitive perspective this book takes a sociocultural approach to language production, looking above all at written and spoken **texts** children produce in naturalistic circumstances. Of course, reading is a very important aspect of learning and social development, covered in depth by many books written from a variety of perspectives. It should be remembered while studying this unit that reading, as all interpretation, is an active process and a necessary precursor to the writing of texts.

Imagine a small girl sitting on a high chair, smearing food on the tray into a pattern. Of course, this might be at random, while the child is making a mess, feeling the texture of the food. Possibly the child is enjoying the tension before the activity is stopped by an adult concerned

11

at possible spillages onto the floor! But imagine you are watching, and notice a distinctly drawn face, or perhaps even the initial letter of the child's name: in these events she is representing something by external means.

The Russian psychologist, Lev Vygotsky, drew a strong link between children's practical activities and their appropriation of symbols that are meaningful in a culture. That is, children seek out ways to make use of symbolic systems as tools, while engaged in processes of improving their understanding. As shall be shown in Units three and four, this approach is characteristic of the beginning use of speech in very young children. (There is more information about Vygotsky and his ideas later in this book.)

Example 1: Oliver

Look at Text: Oliver's musical notes, which shows a pattern drawn by Oliver a few days after his fourth birthday.

Text: Oliver's musical notes

Oliver's mark-making looks as though it could be 'emergent writing', that is the very early attempts of someone who is beginning to understand that certain kinds of patterns on paper represent spoken language. Actually, Oliver explained that he was drawing 'musical notes'.

Vygotsky wrote:

> In the process of development the child not only masters the items of cultural experience but the habits and forms of cultural behaviour, the cultural methods of reasoning.
>
> (1994: 56)

Two points are especially worth noting here:

◎ Vygotsky emphasises the active nature of the child's development; the growth of understanding is accomplished while *doing* things with tools (including symbolic systems) available to the child.

◎ The emphasis on 'cultural' is important. In Example 1 above, Oliver had been excited to find out that music could be 'written down'; clearly this is a particular convention that could only have been devised in human society.

Children make sense of symbolic practices, whether involving images, musical sounds, written texts and so on, through their presence in communities. People create and interpret meanings together. Children learn that boxes of foodstuffs have labels and often pictures that in some way indicate the product within and that assist consumers in selecting their choice. Children learn how to dance or how to draw, partly through watching others, partly through the responses that others make to their own efforts, and partly through the special individually motivated capabilities they bring to the activity in question.

Currently, a great deal of attention is being paid to multimodality in communication, that is the interaction between images, words and sounds employed at the same time. Many people understandably praise the Internet for the possibilities it affords for multimedia communications and it is suggested that children today in the richer countries of the world are growing up in a more 'multimodal' world. Others, when writing about multimodality, stress the lack of division between acting with the body and thinking with the mind that is characteristic of young children acting in communicative ways.

13

Anning and Edwards suggest:

> Young children move freely between expressing themselves through spoken language, mark-making, making models, manipulating objects in role play and physical movements.
>
> (1999: 89)

In the various settings they encounter, children learn to develop specific skills, including communication skills in various channels, and to combine these in particular ways. Schooling is concerned with developing children's repertoires of communicative actions, of encouraging valued patterns of activities. Of course many repertoires are developed in less formal contexts.

Example 2: Kathleen's history book

Schools often approach the teaching of literacy – reading and writing – through working with children's inclinations towards multimodal activities. Specific combinations and conventions are introduced from the beginning of formal schooling, partly through more subtle means than direct instruction. For example, some early exercise books used in schools have a white space on the top half of the page while the bottom half has horizontal lines, arranged not too closely but at regular intervals. This facilitates particular kinds of textual productions (while closing off or at least discouraging others).

Particularly in societies where the curriculum is highly regulated, children are intended to develop their skills in reading and writing according to standards judged by the education system as appropriate for their age.

Activity

On page 15 you will find a reproduction from Kathleen's history exercise book. She was aged 6′ 4″ at this time. You can also see the teacher's annotations.

Describe Kathleen's capabilities in literacy as evidenced by this text. (In what way do you think she might have had direct assistance during the composition process?) Comment too on the teacher's annotations: the 'e's inserted into the heading and ticks in the text. Would you have done the same? What does this text, interpreted in the light of your own background knowledge, tell you about school literacy practices – what is valued, for example?

(Note: there is no commentary on this activity.)

Text: Kathleen's exercise book

Monday   13th November

<u>different</u>

Evacuees were frightened of cows because in the city there was none. Then They had powdered eggs ✓ they are bungalows. they are one Stori bundus stams and Shops. because ✓ they were rele eggs.

Example 3: Kathleen's email

Look at Text: Kathleen's email, which shows an email that Kathleen sent to her uncle in the US two weeks after her piece of writing discussed in Example 2 above. Personal information has been deleted and replaced by the information in square brackets.

15

Describe Kathleen's response to the semiotic possibilities of the channel. That is, what kind of communicative interaction is made possible by email – what basic opportunities and constraints result from the physical properties of the channel; how does Kathleen respond to them?

Text: Kathleen's email

Subject:	ii
Date	26/11/00 17:02:42 GMT Standard Time
From:	Kathleen [remainder omitted]
To:	[email address omitted]

hey this kathleen. martin I have some very good news last week I got a new baeg.

Commentary

If you approach this text in the same way as you did Kathleen's history work, you would be missing aspects of understanding relating to conventions and audience. For a young child developing her fine motor skills, this means a potentially challenging obstacle, that presented by handwriting, is removed (although replaced by another). If one can find the intended key on the key-board, the graphic symbol is presented perfectly to the other person. Spelling is generally just as much under a person's control when emailing as when handwriting in school, but it is helpful to think about intentions and audience when interpreting. Viewed through the conventions of school literacy practices, it is immediately obvious that 'martin' and 'kathleen' should have an initial capital. This instance here may be an 'error' of Kathleen's or it may be that she is already conscious of the frequent informality and avoidance of such issues as capitalisation in emails and text messages. (She had received emails from adults written entirely in block capitals.) However, the misspelling 'baeg' did cause problems. Her uncle congratulated her on obtaining a new 'bag' in his response, whereas she had intended to tell him of her swimming badge. When writing in a schoolbook, the intention is not so much to communicate new information to a person – presumably the primary audience of the book is the teacher – but rather to demonstrate capabilities in schooled literacy. Writing practice in school is specifically designed to reduce and eventually virtually eliminate spelling errors. The email is a direct communication; the word 'baeg' is clearly designed to be the climax of the message, but the misspelling unfortunately created an obstacle in the recipient's understanding at this crucial point.

Example 4: Conor's letter

Text: Conor's tooth fairy letter was produced by a six-year-old boy. It has been reproduced at exactly the same size it was made.

Activity

You may remember that Vygotsky emphasised the role of the 'cultural' for the child's development and learning (see p. 12). In what ways is Conor drawing on his culture?

Text: Conor's tooth fairy letter

Transliteration: Dear tooth fairy i have got a new girlfriend and a new teacher. I am top. but I am not in a new scoool. love from Conor.

Commentary

This text is clearly part of a specific cultural experience. In Conor's society, a myth for children is that if a milk tooth that comes out is placed under the child's pillow at night, the 'tooth fairy' magically replaces it with a coin to be discovered in the morning. Presumably a function of the myth is to mitigate against potential anxiety at losing a tooth.

In this instance, Conor has decided to communicate with the tooth fairy. Since he will be asleep at the time of her visit, the only means possible is through a paper-based message. The text he creates is the familiar combination of writing and drawing, already discussed above. Here, as frequently, they are accomplished with the same basic tool. Conor has taken the needs of his audience into careful consideration both in the formatting and content of his production. The writing is small, appropriate to the size of the imagined fairy, and conveys his news since the loss of the previous tooth.

Conor draws upon a number of specific cultural conventions in his production of both writing and drawing. The genre of letter writing is strongly evident. At the beginning is the formal salutation 'dear' coupled with the identification of the intended recipient. There is a conventional ending, denoting affection, followed by the name of the sender. The body of the message indicates in its syntax and punctuation an attempt to write in sentences. Spelling is generally conventional but with some misspellings in two **orthographically** difficult words. The drawing is highly stylised and representative of strong conventions in the act of representation in children's art (within Conor's society, obviously). The sun and the house are identifiable stereotypes.

MATHEMATICAL UNDERSTANDING

Long before children encounter 'Maths' as a school subject, they grapple with shapes, quantities and numbers as an intrinsic part of their lives.

Example 5: Daniel

A study was made of the production of the word 'two' by Daniel during one month around the period of his second birthday.

At 1' 11" while playing with two bits of banana Daniel said, seemingly to himself, 'nana bit two'. Shortly afterwards came his birthday and the discovery that '2' was associated with him and could be used to label cards, cakes and even trains (in picture books). He begun to say often, on seeing a written '2': 'My two!' It appeared that he did not have an understanding of what two things this 'two' applied to; but Daniel did know he was bigger than a friend, 'Baby Aran' who was, he knew, 'one'.

Daniel had grasped that the 'two' of spoken language can be indicated by a digit. He could not read the word 'two', that is recognise 'two' as conveying the meaning of '2', but seemed to understand that the digit in some way stands apart from the alphabetic system of written language. At this time, while Daniel had considerable cultural knowledge of the concept of 'two' – its significance in his society and ways it can be used, – his understanding of it as a mathematical symbol was **emergent**.

In thinking about children's writing, reading, mathematics and so on, the word 'emergent' conveys both that the child's understanding is gradually developing, and that it is being produced through interactions within a culture. Daniel was encountering many different uses of '2' in his environment that he was gradually becoming more aware of.

Many wise pre-school and early childhood carers make use of young children's multimodal enthusiasms in gradually developing their understandings of the very particular symbolic system of meaning-making that is the numeric system.

Activity

What may children be learning when they take part in number songs, such as 'one, two, three, four, five, once I caught a fish alive'; 'five little monkeys dancing on the bed' or 'ten green bottles'?

Commentary

Of course, without being able to see inside others' heads, we can never be sure what children are learning. However, from repeated observations of the ways children learn mathematical understandings they may well in this activity be developing in the following ways:

1   learning the fixed names for numbers;

2   learning the sequential order in which they occur;

3   learning the 'one to one' principle – mapping each number onto a single unit;

4   learning that numbers are an abstract notion – you can count five monkeys or five fingers.

Also, the rhythm of the song helps its learnability overall, so, as it is repeated, children can gradually come to more detailed understandings.

WRITING IN CONTEXT

Example 6: Morgan

The text we will look at first was one in a series produced spontaneously by a seven-year-old girl. After doing the writing and drawing she put it up on her bedroom wall as one element in her multifaceted campaign to try to persuade her parents to buy a dog. (Two more of her texts are shown later). In the face of strong opposition, Morgan was at this point trying to persuade them to at least allow her to build relationships with acquaintances' dogs. She hoped gradually to melt their opposition to ownership.

Activity

Looking for the moment at just Text: The dog of dreams, make some notes on what this seven-year-old is demonstrating she knows about writing. Then list the 'errors' if considered according to the conventions associated with schooling.

20

Text: The dog of dreams

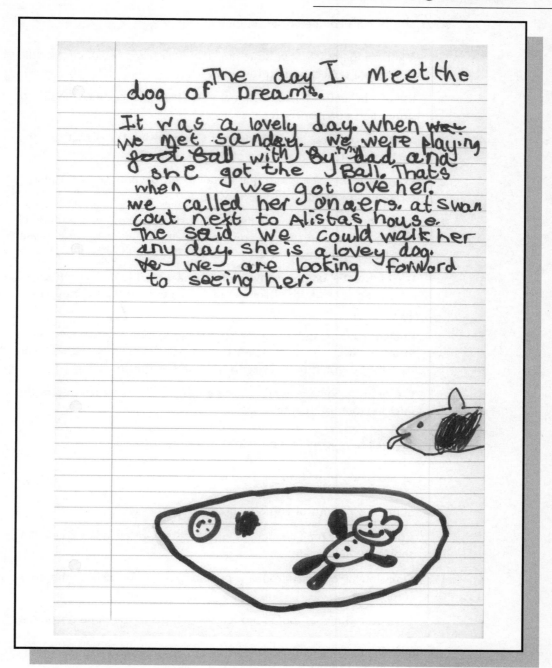

The day I meet the dog of Dreams.

It was a lovely day. When we we met sanday. we were playing foot Ball with By my dad and she got the Ball. Thats when we got love her. we called her onaers. at swan cout next to Alistas house. The said we could walk her any day. she is a lovey dog. we we are looking forword to seeing her.

Commentary

A list of Morgan's competencies might include:

- ◎ A knowledge of narrative structure. The story has a beginning, middle and end (a projection into the future).

- ◎ Use of a heading – a feature of many story-type genres, including short stories and newspaper articles.

- ◎ Ability to compose a preamble – 'It was a lovely day' – that sets the background to the beginning of the true narrative.

- ◎ Considerable spelling skills that at points go beyond 'simple' sound – symbol correspondence (e.g. 'forward').

- ◎ Knowledge of structuring sentences that clearly belong to the mode of writing rather than speech: one would neither start talking by means of a heading, or even be likely to begin 'It was a lovely day . . .'.

- ◎ Use of essential graphic conventions that are used to delimit sentences, i.e. capital letters at the beginning of a sentence and a full stop at the end.

- ◎ Audience awareness – she gives explicit information regarding the dog's location. (If she had no sense of any possible audience other than herself, she would be unlikely to have any reason to do this.)

- ◎ Use of an image and writing on the same page that each inform the interpretation of the other.

You may well have identified other competencies too!

A list of Morgan's 'errors' might include:

- ◎ Some misspellings of English words.

- ◎ Confusion over capitalisation, i.e. some letters written in lower case that should be upper case, and vice versa.

- ◎ Omission of other appropriate punctuation marks such as the apostrophe.

- ◎ Unexpected mix of 'print' and 'cursive' scripts in the same document.

You may well have identified other errors too, as appropriate to the specific standards you adopt when evaluating this writing.

Now, looking at Text: Sandy the dog of your dreams and Text: I want a dog, as well as the previous text, what sources do you think Morgan may be drawing on in her creation of all three?

Text: Sandy the dog of your dreams

Text: I want a dog

Commentary

Although all three texts are produced on identically sized pieces of paper with a simple set of tools, they are quite different in many ways. The first text is an illustrated narrative. The drawing is a view of just part of the head of the dog; the scene is shown as if it is a snapshot during a significant event. This is effective in emphasising certain qualities associated with the dog: her facial expression and focus upon interactions with objects that are placed centrally. The second text is a full portrait. Relative formality is conveyed by the static pose and use of carefully placed captions. The first describes the subject and the second elucidates the name and special quality of the artist. The overall effect is restrained; the emotive effect is indirect in that it is achieved through our recognition that it takes a great deal of care to execute a portrait and that positive evaluation has preceded the selection of subject. In this text, unlike the first, the paper is turned to landscape orientation, indicating the irrelevance of the ruled lines. This is the case in the third text although it consists only of writing and no illustration. Here the lines are not used because Morgan has conveyed the feeling of a billboard poster with large lettering to suggest the depth of her feelings, and a plaintive plea across the bottom ('enewon' being her spelling for 'anyone'). Interpreting these texts, just as creating them, entails knowledge of the genres present in Morgan's society and of the semiotic codes available to its members as meaning-making resources.

Example 7: Bethany

Activity

Look at Text: Bethany's writing. What does Bethany (3' 1") already know about writing? In what ways is her writing likely to develop in the next few years?

Text: Bethany's writing

Commentary

Bethany understands certain things about the physical accomplishment of the act of writing. It appears she used two mark-making tools on this occasion. One is probably a crayon, only capable of relatively thick marks. It appears that she prefers the thinner biro as she has spent considerably longer using it. However, she appears throughout to have carefully controlled her bodily movements in that no marks are close to the edge of the page. When using the biro in particular she has made complex marks, combinations of finely controlled curves and lines that indeed characterise our writing system. In two places she has sequences of two sections of horizontal writing, one closely below the other.

Bethany claimed at the time of producing these marks that this is her 'writing'. She understood that writing is an activity that can be engaged in by an individual with a pen, and writing constitutes a special kind of mark-making that conveys meaning. As her reading skills develop, she will be increasing her knowledge of graphical symbols and be able to practise the fine motor skills, already considerably developed, in order to write symbols that can be interpreted by others. Bethany already has an emergent conception of layout; her marks are not placed randomly anywhere on the page.

As Bethany matures, and perhaps especially as she spends more time in educational environments, she will develop reading and writing skills together with understandings of the specific contexts that shape particular literacy practices. She will learn increasingly sophisticated ways of accomplishing her individual objectives that are both shaped and made sense of by those around her.

Example 8: Brian

From 2000 to 2002 Charmian Kenner directed the project 'Signs of Difference: how children learn to write in different script systems'. This study, based at the Institute of Education in the University of London, investigated six bilingual 5–6-year-olds who are learning two different writing systems at the same time. The research aimed to discover how these children understand the relationship between form and meaning in each system. Two of the children were learning to read and write in Chinese, two in Arabic and two in Spanish, all in addition to English.

Brian is learning to write Spanish as well as English and receives direct instruction in Spanish at a community language school he attends on Saturdays. He is growing up in a mainly Spanish-speaking home, and has one older brother.

Look at Text: A bear which flies, produced by Brian. What can you understand of the meanings he is expressing?

Text: A bear which flies

Commentary

There are three elements on the page. These will be discussed in turn.

At the top left Brian has written his name. The practice of labelling one's work, even drawings, is often encouraged in school settings. This is to facilitate handwriting practice as well as ensure the ownership of authored texts is clear. In British school settings, teachers and parents often praise children's productions, retaining them for at least some period of time. By attaching value to them, adults around the child are often trying to promote in children pride, a sense of ownership and therefore a wish to improve the quality of their work. (The conventional use of the word 'work' here for productions that are not the outcomes of paid labour – the central definition of this word – can in itself be taken as a sign of the value society more broadly attaches to these texts.)

The placing of the authorship label is wholly appropriate to cultural conventions, being in a corner of the page, yet respecting a border of blank space around the whole production. Brian has learnt to begin his name with a capital letter – as was suggested above, the issue of upper case and lower case, and when to use which, is a complex matter (see p. 16). Occasionally adults take advantage of opportunities to avoid differentiation especially in informal written channels such as phone texting and even emails. Here Brian has used the capital letter appropriately at the beginning of the word and then shifted to lower case except possibly for the final letter which has an appearance closer to an upper case version and yet, when we trace the outline, does appear in the process of its forming to be close to the lower case form. The preceding letter is also interesting. The outcome is recognisably 'a' but is a little different from the usual handwritten version. This difference appears to be attributable to the manner of its formation. It is probably safe to assume that the manner of letter 'a' formation Brian is being taught in English is a counter-clockwise near-circle shape starting roughly at top right, followed by a downstroke to the right of that shape, added without removing the writing tool from the paper. Brian is definitely working overall from left to right according to the conventions of both English and Spanish. This is not the only convention of writing systems; other children in the study have to grapple with differing systems, for example Arabic operates from right to left. However it seems most probable that Brian has commenced with a clockwise near-circle shape, accomplishing then a downstroke to the right of the shape, without removing his pen from the paper. It is small wonder that, while coping with the demands for fine motor skills and application of knowledge about letter formation, he seemingly endeavours to follow a general principle of trying to keep his letters even both horizontally and in size. Eventually he will progress to accomplishing the yet more

28

sophisticated demands for slight yet conventionally regulated varying heights for letters, as measured from bottom to top.

Analysis of the forming of this word alone has illustrated both the considerable skills and knowledge Brian already has at his disposal, and the complexity of the challenge a child faces in learning a writing system.

The second element is a drawing. You may or may not have realised that Brian has attempted the very difficult challenge of depicting an animal with wings – it is actually a bear. Charmian Kenner realised that Brian has grappled with the common dilemma between working according to perspective and his need to indicate features of significance. A simplified side perspective view (itself of course a cultural convention, frequently present in art aimed at children) appears in the main body of the animal. However his bear has two wings and two eyes, and he has needed both of each in order to communicate clearly the nature of these characteristics. If he had only drawn one wing it would have been far more difficult to identify this as such, similarly for the eyes. Including both of each operates rather against the 'sideways' view of the overall shape of the body, so in effect Brian has coped as best he can with his artistic predicament. This is encapsulated in the portrayal of the legs. On the one hand these have something of the broad rectangular shape of, say, conventionalised elephants in the sideways view they are often presented in to children, but at the same time Brian has conveyed his knowledge that the creature is a quadruped.

The third element in the text you have probably guessed to be a caption describing the drawing, although it is likely you have been able to go little further in interpretation. Charmian Kenner explains Brian's writing:

> Brian wanted to write a caption for his picture of a flying bear, which could be expressed in Spanish as 'un oso que vuele' ('a bear which flies'). He drew on resources from his knowledge of Spanish and English to write '1osokwle'. The number '1' represented the concept of 'un', whilst 'oso' was a complete word already familiar to Brian. The letters 'k' and 'w' which only appear in Spanish for loan words, represented their English sounds here, but these were also good representations of the similar Spanish sounds required. The final 'le' is the more usual Spanish version of the end of 'vuele'.
>
> (Kenner: unpublished paper)

Overall, the ingenuity, effort and knowledge demonstrated in this production are all considerable. Brian's text is yet another example of the ways in which children work actively to produce meaning, drawing from a broad range of semiotic resources made available to them in their society. The bilinguality of children who, like Brian, are learning more than one language, is not always valued in monolingual societies and educational institutions. Fortunately, Brian's school setting has been wise enough to perceive the advantages of his working towards biliteracy. For example, he is often encouraged to explain his knowledge and intentions in text production. His teacher even encouraged a brief session with Brian as 'teacher' explaining some things about the Spanish writing system and his community class lessons to his schoolmates.

SUMMARY

This unit has revealed that:

◎   Children are active and purposeful meaning-makers, drawing upon the cultural resources made available to them in their society.

◎   Close analysis of texts produced by young children can demonstrate sophisticated knowledge of conventions in their society's semiotic systems as well as the complex nature of interwoven challenges faced by all users of such systems.

◎   If children are given access to tools that interest them, and encouragement when appropriate, they can often display impressive creativity.

Play and talk

Play is recognised as one of the most important contexts for child language, indeed for all aspects of child development. Greta Fein, an authority on pretend play, argues that play is a fuzzy concept, covering a myriad of activities from rough-and-tumble to board games. It is also clear that both the forms of play and the importance attributed to them vary tremendously between cultures. Nevertheless many developmental psychologists, sociolinguists working with children and others have found play a fruitful arena for the investigation of child language.

TRANSCRIBING TALK

Before we look at some data in detail, it could be helpful to consider the issue of transcription: the system used to note down children's speech. In Unit one it was adequate to use the conventions of ordinary written English or German to convey utterances made by Leon, Nadia and so on in order to support the analysis made. Language researchers often want to consider aspects of speech in more depth. For example someone studying **intonation** will need to indicate variations in pitch and tone in their transcript.

Child language researchers sometimes wish to take note of pronunciation, this being an area in which children often display variations in comparison to others around them. Particular sounds may be difficult for children to pronounce, then in turn their attempts to do so may be hard for those around them to interpret. If you have read the core text of this series, *Working with Texts: A core introduction to language analysis*, you will have encountered the IPA (International Phonetic Alphabet) symbols for English phonemes. This is used occasionally in the transcripts that follow in this book where you might particularly wish to take note of a child's pronunciation. You will find a copy of the IPA symbols on p. 87 of this book. Punctuation is used sparingly, to denote prosody. In the transcriptions that follow a full stop denotes a falling tone at the end of a phrase, a question mark a ringing tone, an exclamation mark sudden loudness and/or emphasis and a comma a slight pause. In addition, occasional notes in round brackets are used to give initial information to assist interpretation of the utterance.

Another issue transcribers have to make decisions about is layout. In this book turn breaks are generally indicated by horizontal lines. Sociocultural researchers in child language believe it is normally useful, if not essential, to give some indication of the child's actions while speaking. (This should not surprise you after reading Unit two.) In addition mention is often made of changes in the child's environment, including the actions and speech of others that appear clearly to influence the child.

The most difficult decision of all is how much detail to give. Ultimately, this must depend upon what aspects of the child's language are particularly governing the investigation.

LANGUAGE IN PLAY

Example 1: Emlyn

The following transcription of a family play event was made when Emlyn (E) aged 2′ 2″ came in from the garden to play with his grandmother (J) and a much older cousin, Daniel (D). Later assisted by Grandpa (G), they constructed and played with a train set. This is a transcription of the first ten minutes.

Activity

Look at the transcript of the event shown in Text: Emlyn. What can you say about Emlyn's communicative competencies? What does he appear to have learned in the first two years or so of his life?

Text: Emlyn

Transcription key: In the child utterance column square brackets [ ] enclose phonemic transcriptions and round brackets ( ) enclose additional information on marked features such as prosody, e.g. (song tone).

E's utterances	Contextual descriptions
allgone coat allgone garden	as E is brought in from the garden and his coat is removed
oh!	J and D produce the train set
Daniel [frɛɪn]. train my [frɛɪn].	D and J begin to arrange pieces
where train?	watches D and J make the train set
telly!	as G puts the TV on
railtrain circle, round circle	E points to the circular track
where train gone? where train gone Daniel?	E watches D and J make the track, as yet without the train
make train	E goes and finds train, picks it up E drops the train and plays briefly with the Lego
where train? where train? where train? (louder and louder)	E returns to J and D
where train gone?	E speaks to J and D
	D goes off. G comes over to assist J who is having problems with the track. E finds the train again
wawawawawawa. (singsong tone)	E plays with the train
	J and G complete the track layout and with E put the train on the track. It is turned on and begins to go round
clap!	E claps hands
	J says, 'backwards round circle'
[bækwə] round circle. oh train!	
	G inserts driver as train goes round
man!	

Commentary

You probably noticed that many of Emlyn's utterances are short, often consisting of two words although some are more complex. He also makes one word exclamations or vocalisations that are noises accompanying actions, e.g. 'clap!' or 'wawawawawawa'. The kind of vocalisations that he probably produced since infancy can still appear in appropriate contexts – note, for example, the 'wawawawa' sound while he plays, making something move. The utterance 'railtrain circle, round circle' appears to be two two-word utterances strung together, rather than a more syntactically complex structure that an older person would probably apply in this context. This is evidence that the two-word structure is very useful and dominant for him at this time. However, lengthier structures are appearing when he clearly has strong motivation to communicate. His first 'where train' doesn't receive a response. His second question on this topic is 'where train gone?' and when that is still ignored he tries to elicit a response by directing the question to one interlocutor in particular – a tactic that often works in conversation but which unfortunately still fails this time.

This passage shows one example of immediate imitation: Emlyn attempts to copy J's fairly complex and unusual phrase 'backwards round circle', achieving most of its sounds. Although this transcription is not a phonemic one, it indicates that most of the time E is using sounds in a very recognisable way. Although he initially uses a [fr] sound for [tr] to begin the word 'train', he quickly adjusts his pronunciation. Such adjustments are by no means always possible at this stage, but this example shows that there are occasions a child can spontaneously make modifications, even within a particular conversation. (NB: these modifications happen spontaneously; it is quite pointless to try to teach such pronunciation shifts.)

One interesting word Emlyn uses is 'allgone'. It has been transcribed with that spelling because many English-speaking children appear to construct this as one useful word.

As with all these transcriptions, you may well have noted other points not included in the above analysis.

Example 2: Niamh and Kathleen

While on a caravan holiday in Ireland, Niamh (N), 2' 11", and Kathleen (K), 2' 0", are playing in a sandpit.

Activity

Look at Text: Niamh and Kathleen. To what extent do the girls communicate through language? Are their actions communicative in any way?

Text: Niamh and Kathleen

Transcription key: In the child utterance column square brackets [ ] enclose phonemic transcriptions and round brackets ( ) enclose additional information on marked features such as prosody e.g. (singing). Empty round brackets ( ) indicate short (less than four syllables long) indiscernible utterances.

N's and K's utterances	N's and K's actions
K (to N): ( ) all the sand 'cos it might	N is putting sand in a bucket with her hands
	K picks up a spade
K: do it. [su:i:] time ahh (singing)	K pats some sand in another place N continues to put sand in the bucket then pats it
N: ( ) bucket now	K pats sand near N
N: bury bucket bury bucket bury bucket (singing)	
	K climbs on low wall
K: up down up down (singing)	
N: Kathleen, are you starving?	N is still playing with sand
K: what?	
N: din din time ( ) bucket out	N starts to throw sand out of pit
	K starts to walk away, towards caregiver

Commentary

This episode is typical of many play events by children around the age of two. At first sight a casual observer might consider that they are not playing 'together' at all – they are not engaged in a joint, cooperative activity with the clear rules and roles that appear in games of many sorts. The influential psychologist Piaget wrote that children are essentially 'egocentric' at this age, that is, more occupied in constructing their own understandings than able to engage socially with others.

At the same time, it appears likely that the girls are very aware of one another and that their activities are linked – this is sometimes called 'parallel' play. You probably spotted that actions initiated by one appear to be taken up, although in a different form, by the other, for example patting sand or singing rather than speaking. There is, too, some attempt at directly communicative speech, especially Niamh's question, 'Kathleen, are you starving?' It's not clear whether Kathleen understands the question, although her walk away shortly afterwards might mean that she has.

Play is an important context for language and indeed other aspects of development for the young child. Play does not necessarily exist in the same ways across all cultures, but it seems likely that some form of play is both common and important to most young children in their development capacities to imagine and express themselves. If you have seen young children play, you have very likely realised that it appears important to their emotional wellbeing. Vygotsky wrote:

> Play for a child is a serious game, just as it is for an adolescent, although, of course in a different sense of the word; serious play for a very young child means that he plays without separating the imaginary situation from the real one.
>
> (1967: 17)

Activity

Make a list of some of the ways in which play continues into adolescence and adulthood.

Your list might include many kinds of activities and end up being quite extensive! The linguist Guy Cook considers that play is as much a mode of being for adults as it is for young children. He suggests that our enjoyment of fictional worlds, whether science fiction novels or soap operas on TV, is a manifestation of our dispositions towards play. Guy Cook also points out that language play continues to be important in adulthood, for example in crosswords, jokes and the puns of newspaper headlines. You probably have an opinion as to whether sports – participation and watching – can best be regarded as a development of play in childhood or something else.

Example 3: Nadia and Kathleen

Nadia, aged 8, was driven to a different area of the country to visit her friend, Kathleen, now the same age. While there, Nadia introduced Kathleen to a favourite skipping rhyme:

> Cindereller dressed in yeller.
> Went upstairs to meet a feller.
> By mistake she kissed the snake.
> How many kisses did she make?
> 1, 2, 3, 4 . . . .

The rhyme is sung while two girls swing a rope as the third girl skips. As the counting begins, the tempo is increased and the numbers count how many of the rapid skips the girl succeeds in making before tripping.

Kathleen did not recognise this as a skipping rhyme. However, she said among her friends it was known, but in a different version, and not for skipping:

> Cindereller dressed in yeller.
> Went downstairs to kiss a feller.
> Her knickers fell down
> in the middle of town
> and that was the end of
> Cindereller dressed in yeller.

Children, and indeed many adults, often enjoy repeating simple verse or lyrics in language that is different in style from the usually relatively transparent meaning-making interchanges of everyday life. The playful verses of Example 3 differ from much everyday language in features of their syntax, semantics and phonology. (You might revise your knowledge of these terms if you are not sure of them and consider how they might be applied to this example.)

Just as happens among adults operating with orally shared texts, children's orally transmitted verses often display regional or local variation. Their content is often attuned to children's interests and/or humour, for example through the inclusion of mildly taboo topics.

Activity

Can you remember any childhood verses that are (or were) transmitted verbally? What features of their syntax, semantics and/or phonology make them identifiably playful?

(Note: there is no commentary on this activity.)

THEORISING THE SIGNIFICANCE OF PLAY

Lev Vygotsky, the Russian psychologist already mentioned, examined the development of children's play in the early 1930s. (Although Vygotsky died in 1934, his work was little known in the West until at least the 1960s, and has increased in influence over the last two decades.) Vygotsky was particularly interested in pretence play, which he observed begins at a very early age when the imaginary situation is fairly close to a reproduction of the real situation. Vygotsky referred to an example of a child thrusting a spoon into a doll's mouth mimicking a doctor who has taken her temperature. The child in pretence play in time becomes more used to severing the meaning of a word from the object to which it refers. Vygotsky explains how a stick serving as a horse will begin the process of separating the thought 'horse' from the physical properties and substance of a real horse. Essential to the child here is the motivation to use something to substitute for a horse and the fact that the stick shares certain physical properties with a horse that enable her to play riding.

As Vygotsky and later Catherine Garvey realised, the act of creating an imaginary situation involves the creation of guidelines and constraints on the activity. These are not the rigid rules formulated in advance, that structure the nature of competition in much older children's and adults' games, but rather 'rules stemming from the imaginary situation' (Vygotsky, 1967: 10). They are derived from perceptions made unconsciously about characters, roles, relationships and patterns of behaviour in real life. Children do not of course generally create precise imitations of particular incidents they have observed in real life (such would be too much for the memory capacities of most of us). Rather, what they observe is filtered and shapes their rules of play, to which they bring creative agency and flexibility.

Catherine Garvey made extensive observations of pairs of children playing and produced a useful account of the resources used in pretence play:

(1) Roles or identities, which are assigned not only to the immediate participants but also imagined others;
(2) Plans for actions or story lines, which are often combined to form extended dramas; and
(3) Objects and settings, which are changed or invented as needed.

(Garvey, 1977: 86)

Garvey explains that in a particular play episode the principal spring for action between children might be any one of these: for example, the suggestion that one plays 'Mother' and the other 'Child' triggers off activities in both children derived from their knowledge of this relationship. Or the children might decide upon a sequence of events (such as 'Treating–Healing') which soon brings forth the 'functional roles' of 'Doctor' and 'Patient'. Children are not directly reproducing an event from their particular past but rather using experiences of events real and observed (for example, on television) to construct their own scenarios. Often little or no discussion with playmates is required to elaborate them successfully.

THE CHILDPHONE PROJECT

As an example of a particular field of investigation for examination of children's language in play, we will now look at the work of the Childphone Project. This project (see references on p. 93) has investigated children's pretence telephone talk as well as actual dialogues.

Before looking at children's telephone talk, it would be useful to think a little about the rules for telephone talk, that adults generally take for granted, at least unless things go wrong. As with any piece of technology used in communications, whether a pencil or emailing system, children or any other new users need to learn how to use it. Since the use of telephones is rarely explicitly taught (except perhaps for isolated pieces of advice by expert users), play often features as an element in children's early telephone experiences (see p. 81 for an example of a child beginning to practise elements of telephone use even before he can talk).

Activity

What are the rules of telephone talk? That is, while of course we know there is not a set of laid-down instructions that we are obliged to refer to before deciding what to say, what are the conventions and patterns of behaviour that we adopt in order to communicate effectively on the telephone?

Commentary

First, you will doubtless have observed that there are mechanical issues that vary somewhat according to the type of telephone. However, whatever the phone, you have to know that it is necessary to 'dial' or press appropriate digits to connect through to a particular person's number, that you need to hold one piece of the telephone to your ear, that you need to close the connection somehow to finish the call even if nobody is speaking and so on. As complex as all these factors may be, since this book focuses on language issues, we will merely note that there are many technical issues for new users to deal with, and pass on.

In the 1970s conversation analysts such as Harvey Sacks, Emanual Schegloff and Gail Jefferson began uncovering the highly structured nature of telephone talk. Technical advances such as the advent of mobile phones are altering some of their findings, but the principles behind their observations hold true. In general most telephone calls feature the rules that are laid out in the following paragraph. It's useful to recall at this point that, as with the 'rules' of pretend play, it is not being suggested that these are never broken. On the contrary, any of the following rules can be broken, but nonetheless this in itself is 'marked' as behaviour that for some reason departs from the norm and that we recognise as such.

Rules of telephone discourse

◎ A telephone conversation has definite beginnings and endings (unlike face-to-face talk where, for example, non-verbal contact may begin before and end and after speech communication).

◎ The first exchange is a summons noise caused by the caller (traditionally a 'ring'), responded to by the receiver who says 'hello'.

◎ Therefore, generally it is not the initiator of the call who speaks first.

◎ Each person's identity has to be established to the other early on (this may be done explicitly, through voice recognition, or with the assistance of technology identifying sources of incoming calls).

◎ Some at least vague notion about location is generally shared too (either through use of a landline the location of which is known to both parties, or in the sense that both know they are calling business-to-business, or more explicitly as with 'I'm on the train', spoken on a mobile.

◎ In general one person speaks at a time and silence is avoided (this is a good example of a 'rule' that is often broken for special effect).

◎ The exchange of greetings frequently precedes the main topic of the call but is not mandatory, although it is likely to be appropriate to the relationship between the talkers and thus fall into relatively predictable patterns.

◎ Telephone calls generally lack a visual element and are between distanced parties; therefore greater explicitness has usually to be adopted in referring to features of the environment than would generally be the case in the face-to-face conversations of talkers sharing the same environment. (It is still true that telephone communication is overwhelmingly sound only, even though the first working videophones were set up in Germany in the 1930s.)

◎ Before the closure of a call, it is usual to mark it with a closing exchange, such as 'bye' . . . 'bye'.

◎ Since a closing exchange immediately precedes the definite closure of a connection, it is usual for one party to offer a pre-closing first, i.e. an indication that they wish to move towards a closure that might either be accepted by the other party who mirrors the pre-closing or rejected by the introduction of a new topic.

41

Example 4: Dennis

One of the studies of the Childphone Project took place in a nursery attached to a school, catering for three- and four-year-old children. In this study, a child-sized telephone box was placed in the nursery among the many other toys and activities the children could choose to engage with. A small video camera recorded all activity inside the box, and a microphone was placed inside the mouthpiece that connected to a tape recorder to capture the children's talk. All talk was spontaneous and the children only used the toy telephone when they wanted to play with it.

Dennis, 3' 0", started nursery school during this phase of the project. The first time his mother left he did little but cry. As he started to settle, however, he seemed to particularly enjoy going into the telephone box and making pretence calls.

Activity

Look at Text: Dennis, and analyse the knowledge of telephone discourse rules that Dennis (D) is demonstrating in his play.

Text: Dennis

Transcription key: In the child utterance column square brackets [ ] enclose phonemic transcriptions.

D's utterances	D's actions
	picks up handset
hello	
alright Mum	
I [sɔ:nəm]	
alright, bye	
bye Mum	
	Dennis hangs up

Dennis is recreating one half of a telephone call in his play. He is using many features of the conventional structure of a telephone call. So, he starts the 'conversation' with an opening, 'hello', as is usually a necessity on the telephone. Telephone calls generally feature very definite beginnings and ends, for these starts and finishes cannot be accomplished non-verbally, as they might with a face-to-face encounter. Again owing to the absence of face recognition, mutual recognition has to be achieved either through technological means or through a personal greeting. 'Alright mum' usually identifies both parties simultaneously, while constituting a greeting at the same time. Dennis includes a topic, a main reason for calling, here a variant of 'I saw them' (pronounced perfectly adequately according to his Lancashire dialect). Investigations of large corpora of English language have shown that 'right' and 'alright', besides often functioning as greetings, also often occur as pre-closings. Dennis's 'alright, bye' is quite conventional as a pre-closing signal moving quickly to signal the speaker's intent to move towards hanging up.

Of course, Dennis has not consciously constructed rules of telephone discourse to govern his play; as Vygotsky suggested: 'what passes unnoticed by the child in real life . . . becomes a rule of behaviour in play' (1978: 95). Vygotsky also suggested that play is an arena in which the child makes his greatest achievements, sometimes reaching above his normal standards of language and activity. Sometimes this happens in the context of **socio-dramatic play**, that is, when children play together in pretence mode, using (often negotiating) the elements of 'role', 'plan' and 'object' as explained by Garvey (see p. 39).

Example 5: Megan

The elaborate piece of **sociodramatic play** that follows centres on Megan (M), 3' 6", a skilful and imaginative leader in sociodramatic play. She was sometimes, as here, effective in encouraging others less articulate than herself, both with more elaborate play than they would otherwise be likely to create and in the speech they used. Observations of the children showed that in general Callum (C), also 3' 6", did not have the fluency of Megan. Darren (D), who also features in the following extract, had considerable language and learning difficulties and did not later proceed to the next stage of schooling with the other children. He did not use words much beyond occasional monosyllables. The episode starts when D is in the phone box, holding the phone.

Activity

> Look at Text: Megan. Taking each child in turn, examine the contribution they offer to the play, especially through language, and how this is taken up by the others.

Text: Megan

Transcription key: In the second column square brackets [ ] enclose information on direction of speech and round brackets ( ) enclose additional information on marked features such as prosody e.g. (singing tone). Empty round brackets ( ) indicate short (less than four syllables long) indiscernible utterances.

M's speech into phone	M's speech not into phone	M's actions	Others' speech and actions
	I'm going in	M climbs into box and takes phone away from D	
	I'm ringing somebody up. My dad's at work and I'm going to ring him now		
			D: 'My daddy!'
	yeh!	points outside box	D looks to see where she is pointing. C approaches box, showing his hand, 'Ow'
	what, what dad? [to C]		
			C approaches and shows M and D his hand
	oh ( ) [to C] I'm going to ring the doctor up I'm going to ring the doctor up	dials	C goes away D exits

M's speech into phone	M's speech not into phone	M's actions	Others' speech and actions
		hangs up	
	doctor up	dials	
			C approaches, showing finger, 'It's broken'
	we're going to ring the doctor up aren't we	lifts phone, dials	
			C, 'Who, me?' enters box
	yes cos you've got a broke		
		dials	
		puts phone to ear	
hello doctor			
	she's there now [turning to D and C, speaking quietly]	holds phone away from head	
hello, come to my house 'cos my dad's got a broken finger		puts phone to ear	
yeah			
he's got a broken finger all well and he's alright and he isn't crying now 'cos he's just alright he's not crying			
	aren't you not [to C]	nuzzles C with head	
he's got blu tac in his nails um have to get em out and are you the doctor		holds phone to ear	

45

M's speech into phone	M's speech not into phone	M's actions	Others' speech and actions
		in pause tries to touch dial	C and D also try to touch dial. C: 'I ring it'
			C moves back suddenly holding his finger, 'ow'
		takes phone away	
		puts phone to ear	
he's hurting now 'cos Darren did his finger he went it like – ow! an' he said ow and he said ow		bends finger	C pummels D gently
he did said ow			C looks at finger again
		looks at C and D	C: 'I got broken finger' to D
	I know you have haven't you	takes phone away	
			C: 'yeh'
	got it haven't you haven't you daddy	examines C's finger	
		puts phone to ear	
he's got he he's got a broken finger and he's hurt so and he's OK			D bangs side of box with fist
		smiles at D	D bangs side of box with fist
and he's OK and			
			C: 'Me ring doctor'
			D vocalises loudly

M's speech into phone	M's speech not into phone	M's actions	Others' speech and actions
		puts finger to mouth	
	shush I'm on the phone [to C and D]		
	I'm on		C: 'I'm ringing up doctor'

Commentary

Darren

It was mentioned above that Darren has considerable learning and language difficulties and that simple monosyllables are usually the extent of his speech. At his first utterance he may not have understood the import of Megan's announced plan for the pretence play, but nevertheless he does pick up on the mention of 'my dad', exclaiming, 'my daddy!' – presumably a very salient phrase to him.

He shows some interest in the telephone which is at the centre of the play. He appears to be supporting C's wish to use the phone when he vocalises loudly (without words) when C says, 'Me ring doctor' towards the end of the extract.

Callum

Callum's interest for most of the extract seems to be centred on his hurt finger. (Perhaps it should be added that, to the researcher as to the teachers present, very little hurt seemed to be sustained.) His 'hurt finger' is made much use of in Megan's pretence, causing a switch of topic and pretend phone interlocutor. His 'Who, me?' seems to suggest he is responding to the 'we' Megan has employed in her previous turn: her declaration that suggests that she is not the only person involved in making the pretence call. Although he pays attention to Megan's call, after a while he shows some impatience when the apparent promise is not delivered and tries to use the phone.

47

Megan, with her highly sophisticated play, manages to keep control of the play – and indeed the phone. Callum indicates by actions and words that he wants to use the phone. Towards the end of the extract his linguistic output is at its most developed, and hence potentially persuasive, as he expresses his intention to use the telephone, framing this wish within the pretence scenario involving the imaginary 'doctor' interlocutor. It is interesting though to note that, although Callum appears to have understood how his hurt finger has been incorporated into the play, he has not shown a sign of accepting (or explicitly rejecting) the role of 'dad'.

Megan

Megan's creation and sustenance of the piece of pretence play, only part of which is given here, is testament to her quick thinking and communication capabilities. It is also important as she is shown to be inspired by her partners and in turn to provide a tremendously supportive environment for the boys she involves. She is very responsive to cues created by the others, as at the beginning when she turns from an articulate announcement of her call: this has presented a number of potential pretence play resources including the plan to make a call utilising the toy phone, and the plan of involving her 'dad at work' – a suitably realistic target. Owing to Darren's utterance, suggesting the presence of a 'daddy' at this end of the phone, and the convenient presence of Callum, she shifts quickly to incorporating Callum as daddy into the pretence scenario. Her question, 'What, what dad?', is an example of the kind of negotiating 'turn' in pretence play, because it both acknowledges Callum's entry and **vocalisation** (here an expression of pain) while pushing the play onwards in creating a potential move for Callum (into the role of 'dad').

A truly remarkable feature of Megan's pretence talk is the skill with which she shifts between the phone talk and the off-phone talk. Her marking of the distinction between the two is achieved both through actions (when she is speaking into the phone, and when not – by no means always so skilfully achieved in pretence involving phones) and through linguistic means. Two particularly skilful markings of the distinctions between the two occur when she is 'interrupting' her telephone talk to speak to the boys. After her appropriate opening 'Hello doctor' into the phone, she turns away and says quietly 'She's there now' before turning back to the phone and resuming the talk directed at the doctor. Similarly, at the end, when her monopoly of the phone and hence possibility within the pretence scenario of talking to the doctor are challenged by the boys using a variety of means, she powerfully interrupts her talk with a finger on the mouth sign and a 'shush I'm on the phone' aside to them that is highly authentic.

She is impressively adept at differentiating between the personal pronouns as they are used, maintaining a consistency between using the second person 'you' when talking to 'dad' directly about his hurt finger, and the second person 'he' when switching back to her conversation about dad with the doctor. Megan's pretence call is highly cohesive, with the employment of repetition and elaboration of detail (frequent qualities of many people's informal telephone talk), neither departing from the theme. Her choices of utterances to the doctor are essentially appropriate, being related to the injury she is reporting on. It includes such sophisticated linguistic features as the use of reported speech (with a very pardonable confusion of the use of the auxiliary in 'did said').

Perhaps it should be emphasised finally that such cohesion in socio-dramatic play involving the telephone was rare in data collected in the Childphone Project. This is mentioned not to suggest that Megan was of exceptional linguistic abilities (although certainly she was among the more generally articulate in her group) but rather to suggest that usually pretence calls dissolved into some confusion of agendas. This is not surprising given their essential insubstantiality and fluidity.

Example 6: Callum

The background to this next pretence telephone call follows on directly from the pretence play episode described in Example 5 above. You may remember that Callum (and Darren) were showing some frustration at not being 'allowed' to use the phone within the pretence play episode that was centrally devised and controlled by Megan.

In the continuation of play which followed the extract quoted above, Callum seemingly gave up on getting the phone and left the box; Megan reacted by hanging up. Perhaps regretting risking the loss of those physical beings involved in the scenario, she immediately encouraged Darren to make a call, saying, 'You ring the doctor's up OK.' Darren lifted the phone up, held it the wrong way up and without saying anything replaced it and left the box, as Callum re-entered. Megan picked up the phone and offered it to Callum, urging him to call the doctor. (The extract below picks up on the action about 30 seconds after the ending of the previous transcript.)

Activity

Look at Text: Callum, and compare Callum's linguistic output in the pretence play episode shown in Text: Megan in Example 5 above.

Text: Callum

Transcription key: In the first column round brackets ( ) enclose comments on transcription e.g. (alternative possibilities). Empty round brackets ( ) indicate short (less than four syllables long) indiscernible utterances.

Callum's speech into phone	Callum's speech not into phone	Callum's actions	Others' speech and actions
		takes phone from Megan	
I got broken finger and I – it's going ( ) alright		holds phone to ear	
			M leaves box
it's broken finger – it's			
		dials	
and it got ( ) one on and it got dad one on doctor and dad/that (alternative possibilities) go home and me go home now ( ) dad			
			M enters: 'Dad!'
	what?		
		hangs up exits box	

Commentary

The qualities of the pretence scenario Megan developed so well, incorporating early contributions from her 'junior' partners, has inspired Callum to attempt pretence telephone talk that is explicit and otherwise appropriate to the telephone channel. Remember that his first presentation of a hurt finger was to hold it out and say, 'ow'; here he linguistically extends this as one would have to on a telephone.

The inclusion of salient names 'doctor' and 'dad' is not accomplished in the same skilful way as Megan, but this is particularly understandable when we think of the various 'characters' involved in the drama. Megan did not elaborate her own role but accomplished the extremely skilful evocation of two roles: 'doctor' – the imaginary interlocutor on the end of the phone – and 'dad' played (in her own mind at least) by Callum. A great deal of pretence play focuses on the taking on of a particular role by the individual playing it – a child might choose the role of 'mother' for example and hope for a playmate to respond in the appropriate role of 'child' or 'father'. But if one puts oneself into the role of Callum for a moment, he is expected to cope simultaneously both with his own 'role' as 'prospective patient with hurt finger' – quite possibly further developed into 'dad' – and with the creation of a (non-speaking, non-acting) character of 'doctor' as the phone interlocutor. One might argue that Callum is keeping himself strictly to the role of 'patient' – as we saw in the last extract there was no firm evidence that he accepted the 'dad' role. However, in this example he shows signs of doing this, partly by saying 'dad' at least once, demonstrating this notion is in his mind, and also by responding to Megan's exclamation of 'dad' without demurring.

At the same time it is also possible that the mention of the word 'dad' – by himself of course – evokes ideas relating to the 'real' Callum and his own dad. His final telephone clause 'and me go home now ( ) dad' might be more explicable in this context – and in any event an assertion of apparent intention or wish displays an explicitness appropriate to the telephone channel.

Some readers might consider that the above analysis goes too far in imputing intentions and roles from scanty evidence. Even if this view is taken, it can perhaps be accepted that pretence play can be a complex mode of interaction, a setting in which children can struggle almost beyond their own capabilities to find the linguistic resources they seek to express themselves.

Example 7: Charlie and Callum

This example continues to reveal how the children's language was stimulated by use of the telephone, while moving away from the particular context of sociodramatic play involving a toy telephone as a prop.

In the second phase of the Childphone study, still in the same nursery with Callum and his friends, a second telephone was set up around the corner of the main L-shaped room. The two telephones were connected so that a child could go into the telephone box or pick up the second phone and speak to a child through the phone. This was a simplified telephone system in relation to actual telecommunication systems, in that the two phones were always connected; it was not necessary to obtain a dialling tone or dial a particular number to get through. The voice input from both phones was recorded. As before, general observations of the children's interactions were made in order to inform the analysis of their telephone talk.

In Text: Charlie and Callum, you will see a text of an extract from a call in which Charlie (Ch) is issuing an invitation to Callum (C). At this stage Charlie is 4′ 4″ and Callum is now 3′ 9″. (There were no actions of note during this extract which is why columns for actions have been dropped from this transcription.)

Text: Charlie and Callum

Ch's speech	C's speech
do you wanna play with the Playdoh cos it's set out	
	no
what do you want – blue Playdoh?	
	no

Judging from observations made of the children's face-to-face invitations to one another to play, Charlie's utterances display an explicitness that was stimulated at least to a degree by the use of the telephone. If the boys had been standing together by the Playdoh, then fewer words and the use of gesture and body language might well have been employed to the same effect. Removing visual cues has perhaps had the effect of promoting moves towards unambiguous language.

We have seen that employing the telephone as a communication tool promotes the need to take account of the point of view of an interlocutor who is at a distance. Greater explicitness may be needed when referring to objects in the speaker's environment, in comparison with that required in face-to-face conversations. Some researchers have pointed out that in some ways this distancing has something in common with the qualities required in literacy practices, whereby a would-be communicator has to learn how language must be employed to reach someone at a distance. However, unlike literacy practices, telephone talk does not require the acquisition of another semiotic code.

Example 8: Nathan and Callum

Four days after the conversation relayed in Example 7, it was Nathan (N), 3' 6", who used the telephone to invite Callum to accompany him in playing with some toys.

Activity

Look at Text: Nathan and Callum. To what extent do you judge Callum's contribution a success or failure?

Text: Nathan and Callum

Transcription key: Empty round brackets ( ) indicate short (less than four syllables long) indiscernible utterances. A question mark denotes a rising tone.

N's speech	N's actions	C's speech	C's actions
are we playing with bricks			
		we're playing with bricks	
yeah?			
		yeah	
alright			
	almost hangs up		
	puts phone to ear		
bye bye			

N's speech	N's actions	C's speech	C's actions
bye bye Callum		I'm on the phone	
what			
bye bye			
		where are you going	
to play with bricks		( ) bricks	

Commentary

Nathan puts forward a plan, that they should both play with bricks. He expresses this in the present tense, rather than the future (e.g. 'shall we play with bricks') but this is by no means inappropriate when talking of immediate action. (Compare with 'I'm on my way' for example, which we generally interpret as meaning 'I am about to set off'.) Callum seems to assent with Nathan, for he turns the statement from a question into a positive statement, still in the same tense. After seemingly ensuring assent to the plan, by initiating an exchange of 'yeah', Nathan moves skilfully into a pre-closing. However he does not hear this exchanged, or brought to a closing. (NB: if the transcription included precise timings, this would assist our interpretation further. We might be able to tell if Nathan allowed sufficient time for a pre-closing/closing, before moving to hang up or if he moved too quickly and, realising this, was motivated to pick up the phone again and make an explicit closing.) Nathan tries to move Callum into an exchange of closings, but meets resistance, first implicit in the absence of pre-closing/closing and then explicit in the statement, 'I'm on the phone.'

So if one takes the central feature of spoken interaction as being the delivery and receipt of a specific message, then we might term Callum's contribution a failure in that he has failed to recognise the essential purpose of telephone conversations. But if a less narrow view is taken of conversation as enacting social relationships, then Callum's communicative strategy can be considered as revealing a high level of orientation towards his partner. Each of Callum's responses has a strong connection to Nathan's immediately previous utterance but he seems to lack or wish to ignore Nathan's over-riding sense of purpose that informs each of his utterances individually.

Callum seems to have enjoyment of telephone talk central to his conception of what is going on rather than the achievement of any extraneous goal.

Example 9

In the last two examples, we have seen how play has been a central topic for talk, as well as how the play telephone system has seemed to encourage talk that is more explicit than would be necessary in face-to-face encounters.

In the final example, Callum is again the telephone interlocutor found by Karl (K) in an example of borderline call between the worlds of pretence play and actual dialogue that sometimes occurred in this phase of the study. It should be noted that Karl's statement 'I'm tidying up' is not true at the time it was uttered. However, the nursery session is moving towards its close, which will be preceded by 'tidy-up time' and going to the toilet.

Activity

Look at Text: Callum and Karl, then identify the features of communicative competence, especially those connected to telephone talk, in the language of the two boys.

Text: Callum and Karl

Transcription key: Round brackets ( ) enclose comments, e.g. (coughs). Empty round brackets ( ) indicate short (less than four syllables long) indiscernible utterances.

K's phone talk	K's actions and off-phone talk	C's phone talk	C's actions and off-phone talk
	picks up phone		picks up phone
hello			
		hello	
Mum			
		yeah	
I want to go home 'cos it – when it's time to go home			
		what time is it?	

K's phone talk	K's actions and off-phone talk	C's phone talk	C's actions and off-phone talk
it's eight o'clock (coughs)			
goodbye		what are you doing?	
I'm tidying up			
		are you? what time is it?	
eight o'clock			
		what time is it now?	
past o'clock			
		see ya	
bye bye			
		Karl!	
bye			
		Karl!	
yeah			
bye bye	takes phone away from head (earpiece is further from head than mouthpiece)	you know when you start going home then you get your shoes on then you go ( ) outside	
		bye	
bye			
bye		bye bye	
			hangs up
see ya tomorrow	hangs up		
			'Karl!'
	K approaches C round corner of room. 'What?'		
			'you go on t'telephone again'
hello	lifts phone		lifts phone

K's phone talk	K's actions and off-phone talk	C's phone talk	C's actions and off-phone talk
		it's not really time for going home	
nearly			
bye	hangs up	what?	
	runs to toilets	Karl	
		Karl	
			hangs up
			runs to toilets

Commentary

You have probably noticed many of the following features and perhaps added observations of your own:

◉ exchange of opening 'hello';

◉ achievement of mutual identification ('mum' is accepted);

◉ initial topic explained by Karl, expressing his wish to go home (perhaps collected by mum);

◉ good turntaking – avoidance of overlap;

◉ coherent questions and appropriate answers;

◉ use of pre-closing by Callum ('see ya');

◉ exchange of closing 'bye'; and

◉ attempt at well-formed expressions of telling the time (of course the boys are far too young to be accomplished at telling the time, and it was not around eight o'clock).

SUMMARY

This unit has suggested:

◎   There are numerous types of human activity that might be included when defining 'play'; many of them involve language.

◎   Forms of play tend to change throughout childhood but in essence stepping out of everyday reality in some way may continue throughout adult life.

◎   Linguistic play can involve variations from everyday norms in any or all of the syntactical, semantic and phonological aspects to humorous effect.

◎   Play is an activity in which children may extend their capabilities, including in language use.

◎   The use of a different communication channel, in a play context, may stimulate the development of discourse features and conventions associated with that medium.

The issue of transcription methods was also introduced:

◎   The depth of detail in transcription should be appropriate to the aim of the research.

◎   Whatever conventions are adopted they should be applied consistently.

◎   When adopting a sociocultural perspective, it is desirable to include at least some information about the child's action and features of the child's environment, including people, that appear likely to be significant for the child and that will assist interpretation of their language.

See the core text for the series, *Working with Texts*, for more information on collecting and transcribing spoken discourse data.

Unit *four*

Early words

FIRST WORDS: NINETEENTH-CENTURY STUDIES

What might you expect a child's first word to be? Apparently one American infant learned to say 'Phew!' as a greeting because her mother would say this as she caught the smell of a dirty nappy [diaper] (Hakuta, 1986: 112–13). Many people believe 'mummy', 'mama' or 'dada' to be a child's first word. Certainly parents often decide that one such sound, made by their young infant, is the child's first meaningful utterance. How can we definitely identify a child's first word and what is it likely to be?

These questions have interested parents for centuries and their careful observations have enriched child language research. One of the early papers on the subject that still reads remarkably up to date in its findings is 'A Biographical Sketch of an Infant' by Charles Darwin, the father of evolutionary theory, published in 1877 (you can easily find it on the Internet). In this paper Charles Darwin wrote that he was convinced that the boy's first word was 'mum' and that this meant 'food'. In a letter that year he added that he thought 'mum' 'comes from shutting the mouth repeatedly as a sign of wanting to eat'.

At first early 'words' can be hard to distinguish from other vocalisations. Infants can be adept at making their feelings known well before they are a year old. Darwin noted, doubtless as many parents before and since, 'A small cause sufficed; thus, when a little over seven months old,

59

he screamed with rage because a lemon slipped away and he could not seize it with his hands.' Yet by this age William Darwin was becoming sensitive to language, responding when told, 'Shake your head' or turning to look for his nurse when her name was mentioned.

Charles Darwin corresponded with William Preyer, an English-born researcher who emigrated to Germany and published his groundbreaking work 'The Mind of the Child' in Germany in 1882, having learned a great deal from watching his son Axel.

William Preyer recognised that it can be quite difficult to make sure that a specific repeated vocalisation is definitely being tied to a particular meaning consistently and therefore is a 'word' for the child. Early words may often sound nothing like the adult version of the word, but count as words nevertheless because they do display a match between a specific sound and a meaning. Axel's two words, that appeared consistently from 1' 1" until 1' 5", after which they were joined by other words, were 'atta' which meant 'going' and 'heiss' meaning hot. (Axel's first language was German.) William Preyer realised that, by the time Axel was producing his first words, he understood many words quite precisely. For example he could if he chose demonstrate any of the following verbs (in German, obviously): run, kick, lie down, cough, blow, bring, give, come and kiss. He could point to over 20 specific objects such as a clock, an ear, a shoe, a chair and so on correctly, showing that he understood what such words were referring to.

COMPREHENSION AND PRODUCTION: FLUIDITY IN MEANING

Example 1: Jacqueline

Probably the most famous investigator of child psychology including language development was the Swiss Jean Piaget. He studied his daughter Jacqueline, who at the age of 1' 1" (20) – that is 1 year, 1 month and 20 days – used a vocalisation (presumably roughly the equivalent perhaps of 'bow-wow' in English) to indicate a dog. At 1' 4" and onwards Jacqueline was *only* using 'bow-wow' for dog. However, Piaget realised, through his extremely painstaking observations, that to claim that she had learned that 'bow-wow' was equivalent to 'dog' would be to oversimplify what was actually happening.

Text: Jacqueline contains Piaget's list of when Jacqueline was observed to say 'bow-wow' and what she appeared to be referring to. How do you think Jacqueline's concept of 'bow-wow' was changing during this period? Of course, there is no 'right answer' to this activity in that we cannot have access to Jacqueline's thought processes.

(Note: there is no commentary on this activity.)

Text: Jacqueline

1′ 11″ (20)	to indicate dogs
	to indicate landlord's dog
	to geometrical pattern on a rug
	to two horses
1′ 2″ (3)	to baby in a pram
1′ 2″ (4)	to hens
1′ 2″ (8)	at sight of dogs, horses, prams and cyclists
1′ 2″ (12)	everything seen from balcony – animals, cars, landlord and people in general
1′ 2″ (15)	trucks being pulled by porters
1′ 3″ (7)	pattern on rug
1′ 4″	only for dogs

If you think about it, Jacqueline's mental journey is one we must in some sense often if not always have gone through when acquiring new words. Think for example of the word 'apple' and the word 'fruit'. A young child might have heard them used when actually referring to the same object, so it is by no means easy to sort out what each word means. And then there are two-dimensional pictures of fruit in books, toy plastic fruit in kitchen play and so on – all objects with quite different physical properties that might well be referred to as 'apple'!

It is possible to find some utterly disreputable discussions of child language acquisition (some are on the Web for example) which suggest that children learn language through having adults point at things and give them the right labels which children imitate. That kind of learning might happen occasionally but does not supply a general description of how children learn language. The philosopher William Quine made a famous argument against the 'object-point-label' explanations of word learning more than forty years ago. He suggested you might imagine you are among people whose language you don't speak. Suddenly a rabbit runs past and your companion points and shouts, 'Gavagai!' You have no way of knowing whether she is referring to the whole rabbit, a part of it such as its colour, an aspect of its behaviour such as its speed, or any other feature of the event that is important to your companion.

So the notion that children learn language through being taught labels for objects is misleading as an explanation for language learning for the following reasons:

1   objects do not have a single referent (or label) as the apple/fruit example illustrates;

2   early words need not be nouns – look for example at Axel's early words above (and see further examples below); and

3   children are active learners who organise most of their own learning out of the resources made available to them, rather than passive recipients of explicit teaching.

Example 2: Beth

A study was made of all the words Beth could say at 1' 2". Evidence was conducted through a long observation and interview with her mother.

Activity

Look at Text: Beth. What can you say about Beth's language at this stage? You may consider the following issues, plus perhaps others you identify for yourself:

◎   types of events, things and activities that evoke language;

◎   circumstances in which she uses words;

◎   how she seems to be learning words;

◎   word meanings – how are these similar or different to conventional 'adult' meanings of words she uses;

◎   pronunciation; and

◎   functions for her language.

Text: Beth

Transcription key: Square brackets [ ] enclose phonemic transcriptions. ´ is an optional symbol that can be used before a stressed syllable.

1   'Mummy, Mummy', said while pointing to something. This is what Beth says when she wants the object in question. She also says it first thing in the morning when she wakes up.

2   'Daddy, Daddy', alternative words first thing in the morning when she wakes up.

3   'phone' {actually [fəʊ]}, when the telephone rings or when someone imitates the sound of a phone ringing.

4   'Donal' or 'Daddy' {pronounced by Beth [´əʊnə] or [dædi:] respectively}, when calling for her daddy, whose name is Donal – [´dəʊnəl].

5   'Niamh' {pronounced by Beth as [ni:]}, although the correct pronunciation is [ni:v].

6   'ball', when interacting with a ball.

7   'Nanny' [næni:], when calling or otherwise referring to either of her grandmothers (referred to by surrounding adults as Granny or Nana).

8   'that there' {pronounced by Beth as [dætdɛə] with rising inflection}, when pointing to things.

9   'vroom vroom', said when on her little car on which she can propel herself around.

10   'no no', said when reaching towards something she knows she's not allowed to have.

11   'ee i ee i oh' [i: aɪ i: aɪ əʊ]. When others sing the nursery rhyme 'Old Macdonald' she will supply the chorus.

12   'la la po'. If someone else will sing the beginning of the Teletubbies song from TV she will supply this part.

13   'bee bo', when playing peekabo.

14   'bye bye', said in appropriate contexts, i.e. when she is leaving or others are leaving.

Commentary

First, it's important to say that this commentary is neither comprehensive nor definitive. Any commentary must be subjective to some degree; we cannot be sure what Beth 'means' by any particular word. Nevertheless, some detailed analysis can be usefully linked to some general observations that can be made about young children's early language.

Types of events, things and activities that evoke language

Beth's language is linked to certain events of the day, that have a routine, even repetitive, quality to them. Waking up evokes a language routine, as does somebody around her leaving. Many of these events are linked to people in some way and even to interactional routines. The kinds of activities that seemingly inspire her to use language are those she initiates or at least is involved in (as opposed to those where she is passively watching). This is true of 'ball', 'that there' and some others, although 'phone' occurs when she witnesses something, that is, the ring of a phone. However, there is an implied suggestion that perhaps this utterance has something of a 'perform-ance' quality: people don't frequently imitate the sound of a telephone ringing. Yet this action is mentioned here as stimulating Beth to say 'phone': perhaps they do this in order to encourage her to 'perform' more often?

As to the 'things' that evoke early words: Beth is quite typical in that names of people and relatively small, familiar objects (such as 'ball') feature in those of her early words that are nouns. For many children, parts of the body and face feature as very early words.

Circumstances in which she uses words

This section overlaps with that above, and you may have already mentioned observations that might belong here, and vice versa. However, you might look particularly at the accompaniment of words with actions. 'Vroom vroom' is a good example to look at first. We might not count this as an early word at all; it might be used by a child who is not yet using words but who is consistently using certain vocalisations to express specific intentions or feel-ings. After all, even a small infant might well have different kinds of cries for different kinds of causes, e.g. discomfort, tiredness, hunger etc. As the child develops, particular vocalisations can become linked with some specific circumstance, such as the action of reaching towards something and the feeling of wanting it. This linking of a vocalisation with a specific circum-stance (or linked set of circumstances) is the precursor to language production in the individual and is sometimes called a proto-word.

Every language community has conventions relating to the use of vocalisations that are not quite words but which denote meaning that is comprehensible. In Jean Briggs's studies of an Inuit community, she observes non-linguistic expressions of affectionate admiration towards young children that include 'Eeeeeee eeee!' and 'Vaaaa!' We recognise 'Ahh!' while not thinking of it as a word nor as culturally specific, even though it is. 'Vroom vroom' does not appear in dictionaries, so some might argue it should not appear in a list of Beth's 'early words'. However, much of her early output shows a linking of specific sounds with specific circumstances.

How she seems to be learning words

Following on directly from the statement above, we can see that Beth is actively producing specific sounds in specific sets of circumstances. Somehow she is receiving support from those around her and her environment more generally that encourages her to do this in ways that are culturally meaningful. So it is 'vroom vroom' that is produced when driving her toy car.

Repetition, in contexts that are fun for her, is an important aspect of language learning. The fun element can partly at least occur in the use of music; as we saw in Unit three, nursery rhymes can be helpful in language learning. What is often significant here is their use in an interactive routine; Beth hasn't picked up 'ee i ee i oh' and 'la la po' merely from watching videos or tapes, but in interacting with others in events based around these rhymes and songs.

Most of these early utterances are very or fairly short, being one, two or a few syllables long. This often maps onto the length of a simple word, and is in any event easier to learn than a long word. However it's important to note that words are not necessarily the significant units for Beth. 'That there' is not obviously two words to her rather than one; indeed it is being used by her as a single unit. We can understand something of the difficulties involved in segmenting words if we imagine ourselves listening to a foreign language we are not particularly familiar with. Even if we start picking out one sequence of sounds and assigning it a meaning, we are unlikely to be sure if, in its written form, it is denoted by a single word or a phrase.

Word meanings

In general, her words are used more to identify particular kinds of interactions involving both her and someone or something else, rather than as reflecting the broader adult usage. For example, 'ball' is produced when she is playing with one.

65

As was mentioned above, it is impossible to be definitive about the meanings of very young children's early words. Her meanings of 'Mummy, Mummy' or 'Daddy, Daddy' on waking up are not precisely fathomable. One might be tempted to assume from this data, written down at this distance from the circumstances in which it first occurred, that she was using these words in a very conventional way to summon either of these people. But her mother when interviewed had the strong sense that this could not be an authentic explanation; this first utterance on waking seemingly was not uttered with the expectation of summoning the person concerned. With what meaning we cannot be sure, but somehow Beth was announcing that she was awake, quite possibly primarily to herself, by using these words.

A more conventional use for 'Daddy' appeared when that word was used once rather than in a sequence of repetition and used to call for her father. The alternative of 'Donal' also strongly indicates that there is some kind of firm distinction here in meaning between these alternatives and the 'Daddy, Daddy' that sometimes appeared first thing in the morning. 'Donal' or 'Daddy' are being used to call that person; the alternation of the two terms indicates Beth's awareness that the same person may be called by two names or terms of address, as she sorts out which one she is going to call him by.

Pronunciation

Beth is displaying some common ways of simplifying pronunciation, in common with many young children. In producing shortened word forms, there is a strong preference for an alternation of vowel sounds with simple consonant sounds from a restricted range and a tendency to often delete anything that does not lie within this pattern. She often truncates words, such as [ni:] for Niamh. Her pronunciation of 'Donal' is interesting in that she also drops off the initial consonant, although retains much of the first, stressed syllable. She also shows a preference for **syllabic reduplication** such as 'bye bye' or 'no no', i.e. taking a simple syllable and repeating it. Some consonants are altered, such as the initial sounds of 'that' and 'there'. Often the pattern of such substitutions is consistent to a particular child (and perhaps more specifically to certain positions within words, for that child). Jean Peccei uses data from a two-year-old child who consistently replaced 's' with 't' saying [tɪp] for 'sip' and [mɪt] for 'miss'.

Functions for her language

It is a very human quality to seek attention from others in order to use them somehow in the fulfilment of one's own wants. As we get older, we learn increasingly sophisticated ways of doing this, both non-verbally and through our language. However, one common thread in many societies is to attract attention through addressing people through use of their names or appropriate kinship term. Beth is sorting this out proactively for herself. It is particularly interesting that she has identified the common quality of grand-mothers and is therefore calling both of them by the same word that is both recognisable and within her pronunciation capabilities, even though more generally in the family two different words, albeit synonyms, are used for each.

It is not uncommon for an early word to be used both to indicate wanting something and for the mother. This is presumably because such a common early experience for the very young child may be that a mother is most of the time the closest person and most likely supplier of wants. So it may take time to separate out, as it were, the word denoting the primary caregiver and a general requesting function!

More could be said about the functions of many of her utterances, but a particularly interesting one to note is 'no no' when reaching towards some-thing she knows she must not have. This directly points to the significance of memory in language learning; not merely in the sense of recalling that a certain word has a certain reference, but a broader social sense of memory. In beginning to initiate a certain action, Beth has remembered what happened on a previous occasion this action was attempted – the behaviour of others and how this was expressed verbally. In Unit six we shall see how Vygotsky made this phenomenon central in his notions about child language development.

You may well have used different examples as illustrations under the headings above. Some of the points made could have been placed under a different heading. In addition, you might have made speculations about Beth's language that could be difficult to prove as either right or wrong.

However, you probably emphasised some of the main points such as the significance of her interactions with others, the overall trend towards simplification of pronunciation (in comparison with adult norms) and the active part she is playing in language learning. Beth is a creative language user, not only an imitator of words she hears.

In looking particularly at the issue of word meaning in these early utterances, some notions have proved particularly useful in pointing our attention towards phenomena found in the language of young children such as Beth.

A technical term that can be used appropriately when describing the language of children at this stage is **holophrastic utterance**. This indicates that children are using what for them are single words although that word may be used to express the sense of a phrase. For example, when Rowan, 1′ 10″, used the word '[bɪkiː]' it did not merely mean 'biccy' for 'biscuit' but rather 'give me a biscuit!'

Another useful term when exploring the relationship between understandings, or conceptual knowledge and early language production, is **underextension**. This occurs when a child can apply a particular word correctly to one instance, but is not generalising the word to other cases of the same phenomenon. For example, Lois Bloom studied a child who said 'ticktock' while looking at one specific clock only. **Overextension** is also frequently a feature of children's language, such as when the word 'apple' is applied to all fruit.

Activity

Which feature of a young child's language do you think a parent would be more likely to notice – underextension or overextension?

Commentary

You probably worked out that adults are more likely to notice overextension. If a child uses the word 'ticktock' with reference to one clock, a parent might well consider that the child has 'learnt' a word for clock and not yet realise that the child is only referring to a single object. But if a child calls a banana an 'apple' that is easy to identify as an 'error', or at least a stage in learning about names of fruit.

LANGUAGE ROUTINES

As was demonstrated by Beth, a considerable amount of early language learning may be relatively formulaic in form. 'La la po' is a phrase not constituted by words that may be found in a dictionary, but is nonetheless a vocalisation of fixed function and form that Beth can produce when prompted by hearing the preceding elements of the song. In Unit three

Example 4 (p. 42), Dennis could apply some of the relatively formulaic elements that characterise openings and closings in the genre of telephone dialogue. Beth too, although much younger, has learnt part of an interactional routine, being able to participate in or even initiate an exchange of farewells appropriately.

Routines that are meaningful and fun to a child, such as nursery rhymes sung with other people, can be useful contexts for children to learn language. Repetition (if enjoyed by the child rather than forced upon them) can provide opportunities for the child to gradually upgrade her participation while coming to improved understandings of what she is hearing and indeed saying herself. This is why some young children can sometimes come to a dialogic relationship with a favourite video or audio tape that may be much more fruitful for their language development than passive television watching.

More formal, somewhat ritualised, exchanges that occur in events such as certain religious and festive ceremonies may also provide contexts in which children may develop their linguistic knowledge. Familiar structures to events and repetitions can assist them to work out the meanings of cultural events and move towards participation.

Everyday life too includes a strong measure of linguistic routines and relatively fixed structures. Many of the questions we hear and answer fall within a limited range. The very predictability of many social language routines can assist children in developing their capacities to both cope with and sometimes creatively add to interactional patterns.

Occasionally, apparent linguistic competence in routines might disguise a lack of social capacities that, when all is well, underlie human communication. One language researcher (here anonymous for obvious reasons) explains:

> My son when very young spoke with a wide vocabulary and near-'perfect' pronunciation. The problem was – as it gradually dawned on me – that he rarely saw language as linked to social functions and did not use it to create meaning in conversation. However, he used language a lot – which fooled the medical profession and delayed his eventual diagnosis of severe communication difficulties/autistic spectrum 'disorder'. He knew the second part of most common adjacency pairs used in casual conversation with children, such as:
>
> Question: 'What did you have for dinner?'
> Response: 'Fish and chips'

– which actually bore no relation to whether or not or what he had eaten. 'Yes' and 'no' were just expected responses – they rarely represented (unless by chance) what he needed or wanted.

Example 3: Molly

One day when she was twenty-two months old, Molly demonstrated that she had learnt a valuable lesson about the arbitrary quality of language. She was eating a banana which she was waving about and calling a [nænə]. Suddenly she stopped and pointed the fruit at her grandmother and exclaimed delightedly [nænə]. She had suddenly realised that the same word stood for both fruit and person.

A few days later, her mother noticed that Molly was beginning to move on from holophrastic utterances to simple constructions. She said, 'Do it' and 'What is it?' (each in appropriate circumstances), two phrases that she used increasingly in the next few weeks. Molly had grasped the essential principle of linking words to express complex ideas. This is an insight and skill that will continue to develop over many years.

SUMMARY

This unit has shown that:

◎   It can be hard to distinguish children's 'first words' from the many other vocalisations they make.

◎   Children of course understand many words before they begin producing them.

◎   Early words may have a variety of functions. It is not the case that first words are necessarily labels for objects or people.

◎   Underextension is particularly common, and overextension may also occur in young children's language production.

One of the foremost experts on children's early words is Lois Bloom. She makes a useful summary of the notion that behind the production of young children's first words lie conceptual developments:

Children do not so much *acquire conventional word meanings* as they develop capacities for recalling and retrieving words in circumstances that are increasingly different and removed from their original experiences with a word.

(Bloom, 1993: 10)

Unit five

Communication before language

This unit:

◎ suggests that even infants can be capable of interacting with some meaningful intent with technologies; and

◎ explores ways in which children begin to communicate before they can use verbal language.

BOOKS BEFORE SPEECH?!

Example 1: Max

'Dada!'

spoken by Max, 14 months old, on a number of occasions when pointing to a book.

This was possibly Max's first clear word, a vocalisation used consistently in a particular circumstance. As we discussed in Unit four, by 'dada!' with the pointing gesture Max may well mean 'give me the book' or 'let's look at the book together' rather than simply be labelling an object in his environment.

Books and other technologies are generally discussed in reference to children who are somewhat older. Literacy – knowledge and capabilities in reading and writing – is taught in early school and/or preschool settings. However, as Max's evident interest shows, interactions with technologies can begin earlier.

Even infants may get considerable enjoyment from many kinds of communication media, including videos, TV, recorded audio tapes, telephones and books. As soon as they can hold books, they will grasp them and look at them. Most babies particularly enjoy looking at books with parents. These may often be picture books without words, stimulating sound games (such as matching animal sounds to the right pictures) or prompting joint singing of nursery rhymes.

Example 2: Babies and books

Jenny, an **educarer**, ran a family literacy workshop with mothers and their babies, all under a year old. Her experiences were written about by Anning and Edwards:

> Some of the parents were initially sceptical about starting to borrow books and try and look at them with children of such a young age. Jenny asked them to share books and try to observe what kinds of books their babies liked best – the format (board or cloth), the layout and use of illustrations (photos, drawings, etc.) – and the kinds of interactions the books produced. The infants sometimes displayed a distinct pattern of preferences; although some had transitory favourites. When given the opportunity however, they were certainly able to convey their likes and dislikes to the parents and quickly became capable of holding the books themselves when this behaviour had been modelled for them by their parents.

> Jenny wrote:

> 'The really exciting things was that we, the parents and I, actually saw the babies taking a keen interest in, and responding enthusiastically to, books. As the parents became more confident, the parent/baby interaction around the books blossomed and we saw a love of books being fostered in the babies.'

> (1999: 106–8)

Example 3: Rowan

Rowan was held in her aunt's arms when she was less than twelve hours' old. It was apparent that she could already differentiate between sounds.

Once, when the room was generally quiet and a book fell onto a toy she started at the unfamiliar clang and almost began to cry. But far noisier sounds bothered her not at all: sudden shouts from her brother and sister, a door banging, the ring of the telephone. It was evident that, even though she was only just born, whether or not a noise disturbed her depended much more on whether she had heard it before than its decibel level.

NEWBORN BABIES

Infants are born with superb hearing abilities. Indeed, this is developed while in the womb, when certain external sounds are perceptible. So Rowan, mentioned above, was born already able to distinguish her mother's voice from others and to recognise characteristic sounds from her siblings. Especially important for language learning is the attribute that newborns can recognise **phonemes** from their own language. Although of course they are a long way from being able to recognise words as such, they nevertheless are born capable of distinguishing between different linguistic sound systems.

In contrast, newborn babies have restricted vision, although they are able to see faces a short distance away. This innate tendency is very useful in the building of **affective** bonds, that is the emotional ties between baby and caregivers that, when positive, enhance the baby's development in all spheres including language. Research has shown that babies respond more strongly to faces or face-like patterns than stimuli with similar visual properties that yet do not resemble the arrangement of human facial features.

Another extremely useful 'foundation stone' in the path towards language is the innate propensity of infants towards turntaking. That is, they are born with certain capabilities and preferences relating to the taking of turns. Some people suggest this preference is observable in the way that infants prefer to feed, in bursts with gaps between in which they may look at their caregiver or at least take a short break.

EARLY COMMUNICATION DEVELOPMENT

As we have seen, babies are born with some useful capacities in respect of communication and language, even though they are unlikely to engage in truly linguistic communication for the first ten to eighteen months of life.

Many babies at about four months are already engaging in interactions with caregivers when vocalisations are alternated and expressions, such as smiles, clearly responded to. Such exchanges of positive affect have been termed protoconversations. Researchers such as Colwyn Trevarthen have shown clearly that infants can take initiating roles as well as imitating their caregivers. In the second six months infants are increasingly sensitive to their partners' attitudes to interactions. (The Social Baby project by Lynne Murray and Liz Andrews, recommended in Further Reading on p. 91 is an excellent site for data on interactions involving babies.)

Infants also produce a slowly changing repertoire of sounds that appear to act as 'exercises' for the organs involved in later language production.

Activity

Study the list entitled Text: Emergence of vocalisations. Why might such a list be useful? What might be its dangers?

Text: Emergence of vocalisations

Age of onset	Term	Description
0 months	crying	expression of, for example, discomfort, hunger; may occur in rhythmic pulses
2 months	coo	more musical and quieter than a cry, dominated by vowel sounds
4 months	vocal play	squeals, gurgles, chuckles, growls etc.
7 months	babbling	repetition of a small set of sounds, e.g. [dæ dæ dæ dæ] that gradually develops into more varied sounds, still produced in patterns
9 to 16 months	first words	single-word utterances; otherwise called holophrastic utterances (see Unit four)
18 to 24 months	word combinations	stringing together of words to produce simple combinations and phrases

Commentary

The information given above can be useful to demonstrate to those around children that the quality of early interactions does matter. Some people have occasionally thought that it is not worth trying to communicate with children before they start talking, for example. On the other hand, babbling is clearly a natural stage that children need to go through before they start talking.

In addition, schedules such as the above can be useful for spotting abnormalities, when early intervention might be useful. It is important to identify deafness as early as possible, for example.

One danger of such a list is that people might mistakenly assume that one type of vocalisation stops when the 'next' begins. 'Onset', the term used at the head of the first column, indicates that this is the age at which the activity begins. Even in this respect, there are many possibilities for variance. Some of the most common might be:

1   a baby born prematurely will be likely to reach these milestones later, since development begins at conception rather than birth;

2   some produce whole phrases before uttering a single word;

3   individual difference causes much variation, for example in the time lapse between comprehension and production of the first word.

So, although facts about average development are of some use they should be interpreted cautiously. One study of American children, discussed by Tomasello and Bates, found that about 10 per cent of 18-month-old children were producing no recognisable language at all.

Deafness need not hold children back in language production. Deaf children will babble at the same stage as hearing children. If they are brought up in a signing environment, they are likely to produce their first signed words at a slightly younger age than hearing children. This is because they are not having to contend with the motor difficulties of having to get their tongues, teeth and lips coordinated into the production of recognisable sounds. As they produce their first signed words, deaf children will stop babbling.

SUMMARY

This unit has briefly outlined some of the physical characteristics that newborn children are born with, and some stages they go through, that facilitate language. Recent research has demonstrated ways in which

77

children appear to be particularly attuned to social interaction from earliest infancy. Colwyn Trevarthen summarised his work investigating the capacities of babies and young children:

> Watching and listening to infants and toddlers I have come to the view that being part of culture is a need human beings are born with – that culture, whatever its contents, is a natural function. The essential motivation is one that strives to comprehend the world by sharing experiences and purposes with other minds, that makes evaluations of reality, not as a scientist is trained to do by experimenting to eliminate differences of understanding so reality can be exposed free of human attitudes and emotions, but in active negotiation of creative imaginings . . .
>
> (Trevarthen, 1995: 5)

Conclusions: theories about child language development

Theories of child language development, i.e. identification and explanations of the processes involved, vary. Scholars are still engaged in an intense debate about the various weights, or degrees of importance, to attach to particular aspects of the language development process in children. This unit will summarise some important points in the sociocultural theory illustrated in this book, and give you some indication of other approaches.

Activity

From your reading of this book, suggest some ways in which the environment (including people!) around young children facilitates their language development.

Commentary

You may have picked up on many different examples of this in the book; of course these shall not be repeated here. You might for example refer to the ways in which children draw on their cultural knowledge, their knowledge

79

of semiotic systems, or the ways in which direct interactions with people appear to encourage and make it easier for babies and young children to engage in communicative processes.

SOCIOCULTURAL EXPLANATIONS OF LANGUAGE DEVELOPMENT

Sociocultural explanations of child language development, often drawing on the work of Vygotsky, emphasise that children:

◎ are born with certain capabilities that predispose them to communicate, eventually with language, with those around them;

◎ draw upon the resources and discourses of their society and culture; and

◎ are active learners, who do a great deal to organise their own learning.

Example 1: Robert

You will find below an extract from a recorded interview with Paul, father of Robert, who is talking about his son's interest in telephones, even before he could talk.

Activity

Look at Text: Robert. In what ways could you draw upon this account as evidence for a sociocultural theory of language development?

(Note: there is no commentary on this activity.)

Robert very quickly, shortly after he learned to walk in fact, developed almost an obsession with telephones. He clearly learnt that when the bell went on the telephone, adults went and picked it up and so very quickly he had one or two toy ones lying around – he very quickly adopted similar sort of behaviours. So if the telephone rang he would run to his and pick it up and would then continue to spend time sitting with it clutched correctly . . . .

He was about a year old when he first started to show signs of being aware that the telephone was a device for talking into. He then became quite forceful in wanting to listen to whoever was actually telephoning . . . so for example if I go home from work I phone home to say 'I'm on my way' . . . she [the child's mother] would put him on the telephone and he would say nothing initially but as he became more practised at having a real telephone in his hand he would start sort of grunting and things – the sounds that babies make . . .

This then developed quite interestingly into his regularly now taking – not a toy phone – but a real telephone that he uses as a toy – he now regularly disappears with his telephone and you will find him sitting in a corner telephone to his ear talking to himself quite happily. This could last for five or ten minutes. His communication is still very poor. He has no words – he still makes a lot of baby sounds – but he's talking to the telephone. It's held to his head correctly and the intonations are there – it's not just gabble . . . He is conversing on the telephone not just making noises. He is on his own terms – alright I'm drawing inferences for this and attributing all sorts of characteristics to what's going on and I could be wrong but it appears to me that he's holding a conversation . . .

COGNITIVISM

Jerome Bruner, who wrote the influential book *Child's Talk* in 1983, is influenced both by sociocultural ideas and by the cognitivism of Piaget. Bruner has always interested himself in the effects of a child's society on their ways of learning, and, as sociocultural and cognitivist thinkers alike, emphasises that the child is an active learner. He wrote that mastery of language 'seems always to be instrumental to doing something with words in the real world, if only meaning something'.

Cognitivists often place a great deal of emphasis on children's interactions with objects as important ways of learning about the world. Jean Piaget, the Swiss psychologist who lived from 1896–1980, might have had more influence than any other linguist on your own early education! For example, while at nursery school or other pre-school provision, did you have a sand table?

Piaget's constructivist ideas were particularly influential in the 1960s–1990s (and therefore to teachers and educarers who trained in this period). Piaget emphasised the importance to children's cognitive development of learning about essential relationships, for example cause and effect. Piaget thought that it was very important for children to actively explore their environment and see how things worked. A child needs to understand how water can make sand wetter, how pushing a toy car can cause it to move, and so on, before he is in a position to grasp that words are symbols, effectively providing labels for objects and events as they stand in relation to one another. What is sometimes called 'discovery learning', whereby a child plays with objects, is thus an essential part of language learning. So, playing with sand and water, if you did so, was intended to facilitate your language learning!

NATIVISTS

The most influential linguist of the twentieth century overall has been the American Noam Chomsky. (That is, he has had most influence on all areas of language study, not just child language.) At first glance it seems quite strange that one very important viewpoint on child language development is inspired by his work. For in 1986 Chomsky was invited to deliver the keynote address to the Boston University Child Language Conference: he called child language research mostly wrong, trivial or absurd! Nevertheless he has been extremely influential on many people developing theories about child language.

In the 1950s Chomsky developed an extremely interesting way of thinking about language. He was struck by the fact that children everywhere learn language and that they do so despite the quality of the language they hear. Children hear people speaking as they do naturally, in bits of sentences, with hesitations, breaks and repetitions. He referred to this as 'the poverty of the stimulus'. Furthermore, they might hear Swahili, or English, or Tagalog, and by and large they grow up competent speakers of the language(s) they hear. Also, they seem to develop an underlying knowledge of the grammar of the language. That is, you may have needed to have the word and definition of 'a sentence' given to you at school, but even without that formally taught knowledge you came to understand what a sentence is, and based your understanding and production of English upon that knowledge. You know that 'going am to the shop I' is not a well-formed sentence in English, and will not be spoken. Yet, you also know there are various forms in which an idea might be expressed. For example 'I'm going to the shop', 'Going to the shop, I am' or 'I'm off t'shop' might all be possible in various dialects, as they all preserve central grammatical features of the English language.

More than this, Chomsky considered that the different grammatical structures of different languages are only relatively superficial differences. All people need to construct the same kinds of meaning relations: for example, Subject Verb Object (such as *the woman eats a cake*). In another language the order of the words might be changed, although without altering the fundamental meaning. For example in German the verb ('eats') would probably be placed at the end of the sentence, or in Russian the subject ('the woman') might come at the end, yet the meaning of the whole sentence would be the same. Chomsky's suggestion then was that such changes are at the surface level of a language, whereas at a deeper level all languages express the same kinds of meaning relations. He then devoted a great deal of effort to describing what he termed a Universal Grammar that underlies all existing human languages. (He thought investigating language as it is produced, for example by children, is less important to developing theories than constructing this Universal Grammar – that is why he downgraded the importance of such investigations at the 1986 conference mentioned above.)

Children, Chomsky suggested, are born with brains that are attuned to this Universal Grammar. The clues they get to their own society's language, provided by the bits and pieces they hear around them, 'trigger' their inbuilt knowledge of the Universal Grammar. They then (unconsciously) apply certain rules and representations in order to become users of a specific language.

Stephen Pinker is a follower of Chomsky who has done much to popularise his work and indeed develop it in certain directions. Pinker has suggested that evolution is an important factor in nativist explanations of language, that is that human brains have *evolved* to have the language capacity for rules and representations that Chomsky identified. Thinking about the making of meaning in different languages, he proposes that there might be an underlying 'language of thought' he calls 'mentalese':

> People do not think in English or Chinese or Apache, they think in a language of thought. This language of thought probably looks a bit like all those languages; presumably it has symbols for concepts, and arrangements of symbols that correspond to who did what to whom . . . But compared to any given language, mentalese must be richer in some ways and simpler in others.
>
> (Pinker, 1994: 81)

Activity

What idea does Pinker have in common with the cognitivists? In what fundamental way do the nativists differ in their viewpoint from the cognitivists?

Commentary

You may remember that the theory behind providing the sand table in early education environments is that a young child needs to understand processes and relationships before she is capable of learning the words that correspond to these. This idea is shared very much by Pinker, as made clear in the quotation above.

However, the notion that exposure to a specific language 'triggers' the child's language capacity downplays the role of the child as an active learner.

Sociocultural explanations of child language development tend to hold quite different views from nativists on this and other fundamental points as we shall see.

VYGOTSKY AND HIS INFLUENCE

Many contemporary scholars of child language such as Catherine Snow and Elaine Slosberg Andersen draw upon the work of the Russian psychologist Lev Vygotsky. Earlier in the book you have read of Vygotsky's emphasis on culture, and the significant part he believed play to fulfil in children's development. He explained that children learn through observing, interpreting and participating in social practices, and as they do so they develop their understanding of semiotic systems.

Vygotsky put forward an explanation of language learning as internalisation. He believed that children listen to language used around and to them and start to use it. As they use it, they gradually come to understand it. This is a good explanatory theory for the 'Daniel' data we looked at in Unit two as well as providing an excellent reason for the number games mentioned also in that unit.

An important element in language acquisition, sometimes neglected by theorists, is children's private speech, i.e. talk to themselves. 'The most important stage in the development of reasoning and speech is the transition from external to internal speech' wrote Vygotsky (1994: 68). Vygotsky noticed how young children speak to themselves as they are engaged in various activities. He suggested that this gradually turns into verbal thought, which is of course an important aspect of our ability to function intelligently. Jean Piaget was also interested in children talking to themselves but believed it was a sign that they were simply not orienting to their audience. Therefore this activity simply died off as children became more social. Vygotsky and his colleagues proved in a series of experiments that even when talking to themselves children are conscious of their audience. For example, children drawing when alone, or surrounded by people who they think do not share their language, produced less private speech than those children who were with other people of their linguistic community. The researchers also wanted to see if less private speech was produced by children engaged in drawing and colouring if loud noise made quiet talk relatively inaudible. In the austere conditions they were working in, there was no possibility of, say, using recorded music turned up high, so Vygotsky and his colleagues persuaded a small orchestra to come in and play on the other side of a curtain, in the interests of science! The amount of private speech was indeed decreased. Incidentally, Vygotsky and his colleague Luria sent a summary of their research to a psychology conference in the US in 1930, when it was completely impossible for them to travel, but little notice was taken of it for several decades.

Vygotsky was also fascinated by studies of the brain, a field of investigation that has developed tremendously with technological advances since his lifetime. He realised that better understandings of how the brain functions would enhance theories of child language development, and also in some circumstances assist our abilities to intervene when children have problems.

Another research topic that Vygotsky frequently commented on was the study of primates. He wrote about how to interpret experimental findings on the capabilities of chimpanzees to deal with simple symbols and how these compared with the capabilities of young children.

Some scholars influenced to some degree by Vygotsky have conducted or are still conducting significant research on aspects of child language. If you look on the Internet or in a library, you may be able to find out more about the following, for example:

◎ Catherine Garvey's study of play and talk;

◎ Catherine Snow's work on bilingualism, and how caregivers modify their own speech to facilitate children's language learning;

◎ Annette Karmiloff-Smith's work with advanced brain-scanning techniques to explore developmental disorders that impact on children's language in negative ways;

◎ research at the Chimpanzee and Human Communication Institute;

◎ Laura Berk's study of young children's private speech.

You should now be more aware of some of the fascinating aspects of child language that can be explored whether by a student, researcher, professional worker with children, or parent.

IPA symbols for English phonemes

Consonants

p – pip
b – bib
t – ten
d – den
k – cat
g – get
f – fish
v – van
θ – thigh
ð – thy
s – set
z – zen
ʃ – ship
ʒ – leisure
h – hen
tʃ – church
dʒ – judge
m – man
n – man
ŋ – sing
l – let
r – ride
w – wet
j – yet

Short vowels

ɪ   pit
ɛ   pet
æ   pat
ɒ   pot
ʌ   putt
ʊ   put
ə   patter

Long vowels

i: bean
ɜ: burn
ɑ: barn
ɔ: born
u: boon

Diphthongs

aɪ   bite
ɛɪ   bait
ɔɪ   boy
əʊ   roe
aʊ   house
ʊə   poor
ɪə   ear
ɛə   air

ideas for further projects

◎ Make an observation of an infant who has not yet learnt to talk. In what ways do you observe communication taking place? Ideally, you could return about two months later and see what changes have taken place.

◎ Obtain a video of a child (any age) engaged in an activity that involves some talk. Select any five-minute period and try to make a transcription of all the talk and accompanying actions in that period. You may find it easiest to use columns. Afterwards, write on each of three topics: how the content of the child's talk was affected by actions and talk of anyone else present and themselves; difficulties you encountered in the process of transcription; and anything that surprised you in the transcription.

◎ Observe a child engaged in an activity they define as writing, and afterwards study the text produced. In what ways do you think the specific situation in which they were writing influenced their production? What traces of less immediate cultural influences can you find in the text?

further reading

Abbott, Lesley and Moylett, Helen (eds) (1997) *Working with the Under Threes: responding to children's needs. Early Interactions, volume 2*, Buckingham: Open University Press.
  Also sold as part of a multimedia training pack for those working with children under three, the book reflects many aspects of young children's creativity, from the point of view of those working with them.

The Bilingual Family Newsletter published by Multilingual Matters, Frankfurt Lodge, Clevedon Hall, Victoria Road, Clevedon BS21 7HH, United Kingdom. Email: info@multilingual-matters.com.
  An inexpensive subscription-only source of information, news and contacts relating to bilingual families.

Barrett-Pugh, Caroline and Rohl, Mary (eds) *Literacy Learning in the Early Years*, Buckingham: Open University Press.
  Especially interesting in this book is Caroline Barrett-Pugh's work on working with children with diverse language backgrounds.

Kress, Gunther (1997) *Before Writing: Rethinking the paths to literacy*, London: Routledge.
  A thought-provoking observation of children's early engagements with diverse means of expression. The book contains some beautiful examples of spontaneously produced data, and Kress's interpretations are influential on many contemporary researchers.

Murray, Lynne and Andrews, Liz (2000) *The Social Baby*, Richmond: Children's Project Publishing. See also the website www.socialbaby.com, accessed 7 January 2003.
  A book of stills from video sequences involving babies communicating from birth. Highly pleasing visually and tremendously informative.

Peccei, Jean Stilwell (1999) *Child Language*, 2nd edn, London: Routledge.
  This text is likely to be another useful source for student readers of this book. It provides a particularly strong perspective on the development of word meaning, early syntactical development and pronunciation.

Robinson, Anne, Crawford, Leslie and Hall, Nigel (1991) *Some Day You Will No All About Me*, Portsmouth, New Hampshire: Heinemann.
  An inspirational tale of a children's letter-writing project.

Siraj-Blatchford, Iram and Clarke, Priscilla (2000) *Supporting Identity, Diversity and Language in the Early Years*, Buckingham: Open University Press.
The book includes many brief case studies and practical ideas, and is recommended for those who want to train to work with young children in today's multicultural society.

bibliography

Andersen, Elaine S. (1990) *Speaking with Style: The sociolinguistic skills of children*, London: Routledge.

Anning, Angela and Edwards, Anne (1999) *Promoting Children's Learning from Birth to Five: Developing the new early years professional*, Buckingham: Open University Press.

Augustine (Saint) (397) *Confessions*. Available at: http://www.stoa.org/hippo/, accessed 2 December 2002. See also: O'Donnell, James (1992) *Augustine: Confessions*, Oxford: Clarendon Press.

Baker, Colin and Prys Jones, Sylvia (1998) *Encyclopedia of Bilingualism and Bilingual Education*, Clevedon: Multilingual Matters.

Berk, Laura E. (1994) 'Why children talk to themselves', *Scientific American*, November: 78–83.

Bilingual Family Newsletter, Multilingual Matters (2000) 17(3): 3.

Bloom, Lois (1993) *The Transition from Infancy to Language: Acquiring the power of expression*, Cambridge: Cambridge University Press.

Blum-Kulka, Shoshana and Snow, Catherine E. (eds) (2002) *Talking to Adults*, Mahwah, NJ: Lawrence Erlbaum Associates.

Bowerman, Melissa and Levinson, Stephen C. (eds) (2001) *Language Acquisition and Conceptual Development*, Cambridge: Cambridge University Press.

Briggs, Jean L. (1970) *Never In Anger: Portrait of an Eskimo family*, Cambridge, MA: Harvard University Press.

Briggs, Jean L. (1999) *Inuit Morality Play: The emotional education of a three-year-old*, New Haven, CT: Yale University Press.

Bruner, Jerome (1983) *Child's Talk*, Oxford: Oxford University Press.

Carter, Ron, Goddard, Angela, Reah, Danuta, Sanger, Keith and Bowring, Maggie (1997) *Working With Texts: A core introduction to language analysis*, 2nd edn, London: Routledge.

Childphone Project, the Open University. Available at: http://childphone.open.ac.uk/, accessed 29 November 2002.

Chimpanzee and Human Communication Institute, Central Washington University. Available at: http://www.cwu.edu/~cwuchci/main.html, accessed 28 July 2002.
(Look especially under 'signing behavior', 'what has been learned' and 'research' in FAQs).

Cook, Guy (2000) *Language Play and Language Learning*, Oxford: Oxford University Press.

Darwin, Charles (1877) 'A biographical sketch of an infant', *Mind 2*, 285–94. Also available at: http://psychclassics.yorku.ca/Darwin/infant.htm, accessed 2 August 2001.

Darwin, Charles (1877) 'Letter to A. H. Sayce', (letter number 11077, 28th July) from the Darwin Correspondence Project at the University of Cambridge Library. Available at: http://www.lib.cam.ac.uk/Departments/Darwin/calintro.html, accessed 2 August 2001.

Fein, Greta G. (1981) 'Pretend play in childhood: an integrative review', *Child Development* 52: 1095–118.

Gardner, R. Allen (ed.) (1989) *Teaching Sign Language to Chimpanzees*, New York: State University of New York.

Garvey, Catherine (1984) *Children's Talk*, London: Fontana Press.

Garvey, Catherine (1990/1982) *Play*, Cambridge, MA/London: Harvard University Press/Fontana Press.

Gee, James P. (1996) *Social Linguistics and Literacies: Ideology in discourses*, 2nd edn, London: Taylor and Francis.

Gillen, Julia (1997) '"Couldn't put Dumpty together again": the significance of repetition and routine in young children's language development', in Lesley Abbott and Helen Moylett (eds) *Working with the Under Threes: Responding to children's needs. Early Interactions, Volume 2*, Buckingham: Open University Press, pp. 90–101.

Gillen, Julia (2000) '"It's not really time for going home": three- and four-year-old children learning to talk on the telephone', in Malcolm Coulthard, Janet Cotterill and Frances Rock (eds) *Working with Dialogue: Selected Papers from the 7th IADA Conference, Birmingham 1999*, Tubingen: Max Niemeyer Verlag GmbH, pp. 226–40.

Gillen, Julia (2000) 'Listening to young children talking on the telephone: a reassessment of Vygotsky's notion of "egocentric speech"', *Contemporary Issues in Early Childhood* 1(2): 171–84. (This journal is online at www.triangle.co.uk/CIEC.)

Gillen, Julia (2000) 'Recontextualization: the shaping of telephone discourse in play by three- and four-year-olds', *Language and Education* 14(4): 250–65.

Gillen, Julia (2000) 'Versions of Vygotsky', *British Journal of Educational Studies* 48(2): 183–98.

Gillen, Julia (2001) ' "Is that the little pig?" – using toy telephones in the Early Years classroom' in Prue Goodwin (ed.) *The Articulate Classroom*, London: David Fulton, pp. 93–9.

Gillen, Julia (2002) 'Moves in the territory of literacy? – the telephone discourse of three- and four-year-olds', *Journal of Early Childhood Literacy* 2(1): 21–43.

Hakuta, Kenji (1986) *Mirror of Language: The debate on bilingualism*, New York: Basic Books.

Hall, Nigel (1987) *The Emergence of Literacy*, Sevenoaks: Hodder and Stoughton.

Karmiloff, Kyra and Karmiloff-Smith, Annette (2002) *Pathways to Language*, Cambridge, MA: Harvard University Press.

Karmiloff-Smith, Annette (1984/1985) *Baby It's You*, London: Ebury Press.

Kenner, Charmian (2002) 'Helping pupils to write in more than one language', *Five to Seven*, 2(1): 16–18.

Kenner, Charmian and Gregory, Eve (2003) 'Becoming biliterate', in Nigel Hall, Joanne Larson and Jackie Marsh (eds) *Handbook of Early Childhood Literacy Research*, London: Sage.

Pinker, Stephen (1994) *The Language Instinct*, London: Penguin.

Quine, William V.O. (1960) *Word and Object*, Cambridge, MA: MIT Press.

Rogoff, Barbara (1990) *Apprenticeship in Thinking: Cognitive development in social context*, New York: Oxford University Press.

Rommetveit, Ragnar (1992) 'Outlines of a dialogically based social-cognitive approach to human cognition and communication', in Astri H. Wold (ed.) *The Dialogical Alternative: Towards a theory of language and mind*, Oxford/ Oslo: Oxford University Press/ Solidus Scandinavian University Press.

Sacks, Harvey, Schegloff, Emanuel and Jefferson, Gail (1974) 'A simplest systematics for the organisation of turn-taking for conversation', *Language* 50: 696–735.

Schegloff, Emanuel (1968) 'Sequencing in conversational openings', *American Anthropologist* 70(6): 1075–95.

Schegloff, Emanuel (1979) 'Identification and recognition in telephone conversation openings', in George Psathas (ed.) *Everyday Language*, New York: Irvington.

Schegloff, Emanuel and Sacks, Harvey (1973) 'Opening up closings', *Semiotica* 7: 289–327.

Scollon, Ron (2001) *Mediated Discourse: The nexus of practice*, London: Routledge.

Tomasello, Michael and Bates, Elizabeth (eds) (2001) *Language Development: The essential readings*, Oxford: Blackwell.

Trevarthen, Colwyn (1995) 'The child's need to learn a culture', *Children & Society* 9(1): 5–19.

Vygotsky, Lev S. (1967) 'Play and its role in the mental development of the child', *Soviet Psychology* 5: 6–18.

Vygotsky, Lev S. (1978) *Mind in Society: The development of higher psychological processes*, Michael Cole, Vera John-Steiner, Sylvia Scribner and Ellen Souberman (eds), Cambridge, MA: Harvard University Press.

Vygotsky, Lev S. (1994) 'The problem of the cultural development of the child', in René Van der Veer and Jaan Valsiner (eds) *The Vygotsky Reader*, Oxford: Blackwell.

Humour

Melanie (age 6, bilingual German & American): If and when I die, I will not die in Germany.

Mother (puzzled): Why?

Melanie: Because in Germany you can ONLY go to the Himmel. Look at all the birds, planes, and clouds flying around! It is too busy! In America I can go to Heaven – there it is nice and quiet!

(The German language has only one word for sky and heaven = Himmel.)

Diane Kisling, Germany.

Source: From *The Bilingual Family Newsletter* (2000) 17(3): 3.

index of terms

affective 75

Relating to emotional aspect of expression (either bodily or linguistic).

cognitive processes 3

Mental activities, located in the brain of the individual.

developmental trajectory 3

Direct progression from initial start to final completion.

educarer 74

Professional worker with young children, involved in both their care and education.

emergent 19

Expanding in understanding/knowledge (through activity).

genre 8

A term describing the patterning and conventions of a style of communication. Sometimes writers apply the term only to written communications, but others, following the semiotician Mikhail Bakhtin, apply it also to oral channels. Genres are often characterisable by relatively formulaic beginnings and endings, and increased flexibility in the content of the body of the message. Structural and other constraints apply throughout, identifying the genre, even while often in actual texts creative features occur that breach some of the genre's specific patterns and conventions. Therefore, the nature of genres is often that they are continuously evolving.

holophrastic utterance 68

Something said by a young child at the 'one-word stage' that may sound like a single word but is in fact the compression of a broader idea.

infants 3

In child development literature, this term is normally used to refer to children under the age of one. (In the UK education system, it refers to school children under about seven years of age.)

intonation 31

The process of stressing particular words and phrases by means of pitch and tone of voice.

lexicon 8

Vocabulary.

multimodality 11

Multimodality refers to the integration of different semiotic codes in text, e.g. written or spoken language with pictures, music, gestures etc. This is in essence a feature of every text rather than a new phenomenon. However, the term 'multimodality' has been developed in contemporary times as technological advances have facilitated new communication phenomena.

orthography 18
Conventional writing system, particularly in respect of correct spellings.

overextension 68
Applying a word too broadly, for example calling all men 'dad'.

phoneme 75
The smallest element in the sound system of a language that can display contrast, e.g. compare the initial sounds of *b*in and *d*in.

phonological 8
Relating to linguistic sounds. (Also phonology, the study of sounds in a language.)

psycholinguistics 3
Study of the relationship between use of language and underlying mental processes.

semantic 8
Relating to word meaning.

semiotic 8
Relating to human communication by means of signs and symbols.

sociocultural 3
Relating to culture and social relations; a theoretical perspective that emphasises these.

sociodramatic play 43
Pretence play involving at least two children using in combination any or all of roles, events, objects and settings, imaginatively transformed.

syllabic reduplication 66
The repetition of a simple sound, e.g. "dada". Early words often appear in this form, for which very young children show a strong preference.

syntax 8
Grammatical arrangement of words indicating their connection and relation.

text 11
Traditionally used of a piece of writing but nowadays increasingly used of spoken language too.

underextension 68
Applying a word too narrowly, e.g. 'car' for toy cars but not cars on the road or representations of cars.

universal trajectory 3
Straight path followed by everyone.

utterance 5
Piece of spoken language. Unlike written prose (usually) it is unlikely to fall into sentences.

vocalisation 48
Any sound produced by the mouth, whether linguistic or not (e.g. crying, cooing).